T0171659

Reflections of a Life

ALLEN GILBERTSON

Editor Keith Gilbertson

authorHOUSE®

AuthorHouse™
1663 Liberty Drive
Bloomington, IN 47403
www.authorhouse.com
Phone: 1 (800) 839-8640

Published by AuthorHouse 02/22/2016

ISBN: 978-1-5049-8068-5 (sc)
ISBN: 978-1-5049-8067-8 (e)

Print information available on the last page.

Contents

The wonder of the world,
The beauty and the power,
The shape of things,
Their colors, lights,
And shades: these I saw.
Look ye also while life lasts.
Denys James Watkins-Pitchford
From "Wild Lone, The Story of a Pytchley Fox"

Note to Readers

Everyone has a story....

First of all I am not a writer, just a story teller. This telling may not always have the luxury of proper sentence structure though I consider myself well-read and think I am fair at putting words together that make some sense.

My main inspiration for this long undertaking came from reading the short four page family biography that Esten Rear, the brother of my great grandmother Sara Rear, wrote in 1923. As interesting as it was, I saw it as just an outline with countless personal stories throughout his life missing from between the lines. There should have been much more for us who came later to learn about and enjoy from his life.

My inspiration for having this published in book form came from my Uncle Verdie Gilbertson and my cousin Keith Gilbertson who pushed me to make a book from my notebook and make it more than something for just my descendants to read.

Initially my writings are somewhat stilted and brief but take on more substance as my stories come out. I realize that my brothers may remember some of these stories differently but these are strictly my memories. Memories tend to emphasize peaks and valleys of life at the expense of the great level plain between them and unfortunately the day to day tedium is just not remembered.

I did take certain liberties with some bad and crude language in the description of things and events and for that I do not apologize as that was/is just me!

Esten Rear, ended his short autobiography with the following sentence and that I will echo. "If you make use of some of my rambling, good and well, if not, put it in the wastebasket." It also works fine for me!

Chapter 1

Early Days

When we lived "by Haydenville"

I was born in the Appleton, Minnesota hospital on the 27th of February in 1948 to my parents Roy and Eleanor (Weckhorst) Gilbertson. My dad Roy was the son of Gerhard and Selma (Falla) Gilbertson and the grandson of Jens and Sarah (Rear) Gilbertson and Andrew and Caroline (Olson) Falla. My mother Eleanor was the daughter of Carl and Emma (Skordahl) Weckhorst and the granddaughter of Gustav and Anna (Halversen) Weckhorst and Evan and Turena (Olson) Skordahl.

Some of the earliest memories of my life were when we lived on the farm by Haydenville, which was about five or six miles west of Madison. Haydenville was only a few houses and an elevator that I went to with Dad on occasion. I was maybe four at the time.

Lynn is in the high chair. I am standing behind
our sister Nancy by Haydenville.

On one trip there, I had a rope that Dad gave me to lasso things with and that I really had fun with. We were in the office or main room there, I had my rope, and there were two older boys there also. Somehow, I was left alone with them and one of them grabbed my rope from me and disappeared with it. He came back a few minutes later and had somehow put the rope into a device that braided twine, which ruined my rope. I guess that was my first time being bullied. I don't remember much about the farm itself. Just small visionary snapshots of the house and the barn.

I had a toy pistol and holster and played with it a lot (as old pictures attest!). Hugh Aikens, a hired man of Dad would come over every so often, and he used to bring over a .22 caliber pistol and shoot it. He saw my toy holster and tried his pistol in it and it must have fit and that was the last I saw of my holster! He probably "told" me not to tell Mom and Dad or I'm sure it would have been returned. Hugh had only one leg having lost the other one to the war in Germany and was drunk most of the time while he was over working at our place.

Me "packing heat" about 1953 when I was five

When I was three years old I got appendicitis and had to have an operation to remove it. Mom said that it was close to bursting, and back then could have been fatal! I had the operation in the Madison hospital, and can still clearly remember trying to run away from the nurse, who was trying to put me on a gurney to take me to the operating room. And then trying to fight off the ether mask. Obviously a very significant event in my young life. I was kind of proud of the incision scar when showing it to other kids, as that didn't happen much to young ones.

One time I went with Dad to Madison in our old pickup truck in the winter. As we drove by the courthouse to turn on Main Street a bunch of teenagers started peppering our truck with snowballs! Dad got so mad that he stopped the truck and took off chasing them for a short distance and hollering at them. He never caught any of them!

One more incident that affected me for years was when Mom and Dad dropped Nancy and I off at the *Grand Theater* in Madison to go to a movie. I can't remember the name, it being the first movie of my life. It was a movie about African jungles and huge apes and it scared me so bad I ran out of the theater with Nancy on my heels. When Mom and Dad showed back up to get us, we were sitting on the curb, with me crying and Nancy mad at me that I wouldn't go back in. I had bad dreams for years after that too. Many years later I happened on that same movie playing on TV and couldn't believe how I could be scared by it, but then I was only 3 or 4 years old at the time.

With my sister Nancy

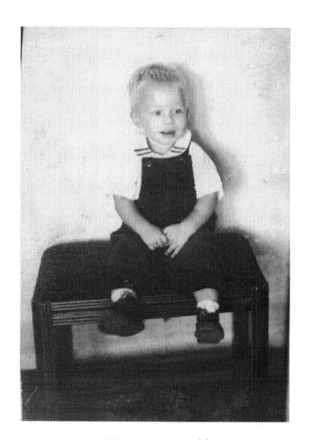

Me at two years old

Chapter 2

Olaf's Farm

Nancy holding Ron, Me and Lynn in 1954 in Montevideo.

In 1952 we moved to "Olaf's farm" which was about 9 miles north and 1 ½ miles east of Montevideo. Olaf Nøkleby owned it and Dad rented it for farming.

Chester and Marlyn Rud and their children Jane, Jerry and Judy lived across the road from us and we visited with them a lot. Usually during these visits us kids played "dress-up" where we would put on old clothes of our parents that were "stored" in old boxes in a "junk" room or attic. The clothes were all too big for us but we had great fun trying out different styles to parade in front of our parents. There were coats, suits, pants, dresses, nylons and hats to wear. These same clothes were also usually worn by our parents when we went "Yule bokking" over the Christmas holidays, but that is another story.

We had a pet or semi-tame deer that spent most of a year with us too. Dad apparently found it as a fawn out in a field and brought it home. Its mother had been killed somehow I suppose. We had an empty wood corn crib that it stayed in and we of course named it "Bambi". I remember playing with it in our yard. One day it disappeared and we never saw it again.

L-R Jerry Rud, Ronnie, Me with a big Bass and Jane
Rud with Crappie. Chester Rud is in the back. Fishing
was good at Lac Qui Parle by the Milan Bridge.

We had this big white rooster that was mean as hell to us kids when Mom or Dad weren't around. It would chase us and peck us any chance it got. We were scared to be out alone because of it. Dad would tell me not to be scared of it because it then senses fear and will pick on us more. "Hit it with a stick" he would say. Ha! One day it did come after me when I was playing with an old ball bat. Anyway, as it flew up at me, I nailed it with the bat or stick, and it ran off and never bothered me again! I can't remember though if it left Nancy, Lynn or Ronnie alone after that.

One day I drank part of a 7-Up bottle of gasoline. Boy was that stupid! I actually thought it was pop even though it was on a shelf in the shed and covered with dust and I sure got pretty sick from it. One life gone!

The day I knocked Dad unconscious was probably a pretty ordinary day until this happened! I was maybe five or six and had this old pitchfork handle that I played with. It was about four feet long and made of heavy ash wood. Dad and I were down at the haystack on the other side of the barn and Dad was forking hay in the pasture for the cattle and I was throwing the pitchfork handle around like a spear. Well, I threw it over the haystack somehow and heard a "thud", actually two "thuds". One was the handle hitting Dad in the head. The other was Dad hitting the ground! I went around the haystack to investigate and there lay Dad. Out cold!

I got so scared I ran up to the house and hid inside someplace, not saying a thing about it to Mom. A little while later here comes Dad to the house and I could hear him asking where I was. I just knew I was going to catch hell then, but when I finally came out, he was okay about it. He didn't know what hit him till he saw my pitchfork handle laying by him. It got to be an event that used to get lots of laughs.

The day I got knocked out, was a little different. Dad was picking corn on a field by Grussings farm and I was along to spread the corn cobs out in the wagon as they were coming out of the corn picker chute. The wagon was full and I was on top of the wagon when Dad turned at the end of the corn row and the corn picker elevator hit me from the side and knocked me off the wagon to the ground. About 8-10 foot fall. The next thing I know, we were on the way home. Dad was worried I may have been hurt bad but I was just bruised up from the fall and scared. Don't think we even went to the doctor.

More on the Grussings farm. They lived ½ mile away in this big Quonset house/chicken house/barn and all under one roof. What I remember about it was that everything in their house, including food, smelled like a chicken house. They were obviously used to it, but we were there for lunch one day and everything either smelled or tasted like chicken shit! I remember Mom and Dad and others laughing about how they lived. There was only one door between them and the chicken house part, and through another door was the cattle barn.

We had this large slough on our land which was very popular for duck hunting. In the fall, Dad would go out with other guys to shoot ducks, and I got to go with him. One time we were on the other side of the slough and I guess I got bored and wanted to go home. So Dad told me to go by myself and to go back the way we came out there. Being a kid, I had forgot the way and although I could see our barn I was lost!

Most of the slough grass and cat tails were taller than me so nothing looked familiar. I soon got into a spot where there was all water around me and so I panicked and started wading into the water which was over my waist, heading to where I was hoping home was. I finally showed up at the house completely wet and covered with stinky slough mud and Mom was furious. I believe Dad caught hell over that and I can't remember going out there hunting again! That slough no longer exists. It was eventually drained for crop land. Poor ducks!

The slough was also where Nancy and I first learned to ice skate! We had these old secondhand, or more, skates that had never been sharpened and that we would pack the toe end with tissues or toilet paper so they would fit somewhat. Then we would put them on at the house and walk on the blades through the pasture and plowed fields to get to the ice! We never knew what it was like to skate on sharp blades because no one else had sharp blades either. That concept was beyond us! We had lots of fun skating though and sometimes neighbors or cousins would come over to skate too.

We would sometimes visit James and Pearl Ryer and their children Wendell, Genie, Jerry and Marsha. (Pearl was my grandmother Selma's sister.) They lived about a mile away. This one winter there was lots of snow and in their yard by the house the snowdrifts were almost up to the roof. Jerry, their youngest son was about 4 years older than me and had tunneled out a huge snow fort under the snow, which was so hard you could walk on it. He had rooms and tunnels under it that I could walk upright in. We had great fun in it while it lasted. I wasn't big enough to make something like that myself. Jerry later played in a band that played in one of the beer joints in Montevideo. My cousin Gary and I used to sneak in there sometimes on Friday shopping trips to town, to watch him play till we got kicked out.

I started first grade while living on Olaf's farm. The old one room schoolhouse was called District 31 and was about a mile and a half northwest from our farm and close to the Ryer farm. A notable fact of this school was that many of the Falla children went there as young children. Grandma Selma Falla and Grandpa Gerhard Gilbertson went there too. One of the founders of District 31 was my Great Grandpa Jens Gilbertson.

Anyway that's where my education started. I can't remember who all was in my class other than Larry Myhre who I also graduated from Milan High School with and there was one or two others.

The one thing about one room school houses, other than close camaraderie, is that we learned from not only our own classes at the front with the teacher, but that we learned either consciously or subconsciously from the other classes going on up front. What a great time.

During recess the whole school generally played together at various games like kickball, Annie-I-over, pom, pom pull away, or in the winter, ice skating! Like we did at home, we skaters would put our skates on in the schoolhouse, walk across the gravel road, about ¼ mile over a plowed field to a small pond, where we would skate for only a short time before the recess bell would ring, then back over the field to the schoolhouse again. I wish I still had those old skates to see what the blades looked like!

Our teacher was Mrs. Brown and all I can remember about her is that she would sometimes bring a raw onion for lunch, and eat it like an apple!

While school was in session when we had to go to the outhouse we had to raise our hand with either one or two fingers raised. One for peeing and two if we had to poop. I never understood what difference that made but it must have been tradition! Hence number two. And why did the teacher have to know from the front or from the butt anyway? I was bashful to the extreme and the first time I had to pee I was scared to raise my hand so I held it and held it till I couldn't anymore. So I sat there at my front row desk and peed my pants. When it overflowed the curved desk seat it dripped on the floor, and being an old building it had a slight lean to the back, and my pee was slowly running under other kids' desks to the rear of the room.

Finally an older kid noticed his shoes in pee, saw where it was coming from and told the teacher. She stopped the class she was teaching and walked me to the back, in front of everyone of course, and there I stayed till school let out. The worst part was that Grussings were going to give Nancy and I a ride home that day and I had to sit on some old feed sacks while they teased me all the way home. I don't think I ever peed my pants in school again!

With our 1951 Ford at Olaf's farm. Ronnie is the baby in Mom's arm and I am holding on to Lynn.

One of our family outings used to be going to the small town of Watson to see the outdoor movie that played there on Saturday nights. It was quite a social event and there were always lots of people. They had a screen set up between two stores on Main Street, the two stores being the side walls of the outdoor theater. People usually sat on the ground and either watched the movie or visited with friends while the kids ran wild. The movies were all black and white too.

Dad had an old exposed hammer double-barreled shotgun on the farm. Somehow this gun disappeared one year and Dad couldn't figure out what happened to it or who borrowed it or whatever. Some years after we left that farm, someone, I can't remember who, came to our place with the shotgun and said that he found it in the granary on Olaf's farm, leaning against a wall in a corner. Dad had evidently forgot he stood it there before he filled the granary with oats! Well the gun was covered for several years till the grain was sold. Preserved perfectly in the dry grain. We got the shotgun back, still to shoot more ducks and pheasants and it is now in my youngest brother Ron's possession.

Chapter 3

Living in Montevideo

We moved into Montevideo after my Dad and his brother Curtis started a television retail store together. Our hose was one block west of Ramsey Elementary school and that is where I started 2nd grade. What a difference to go to a school with 25 or 30 other kids and they were all in the same grade!

Farm living was fun but living in town was a lot more exciting at that age. Other kids to play with every day and that meant more trouble to get into. We were constantly exploring new territory and every week it seemed, we dared to go a little farther from home.

One older kid had a powerful bow that could shoot arrows up and out of sight. One day we were all out in this open field by our house and he was shooting arrows up and we tried to guess where they would come down. My brother Lynn was out there too and maybe four years old at the time. Up went another arrow and looked like it might land near us. I just happened to grab Lynn and pull him back to me and down came the arrow on the same spot where Lynn was standing earlier! He just missed being hurt real bad, or worse!

We went to lots of movies with Mom and Dad when we were young and we still enjoy going out to movies to this day. We were also just as affected by movies and movie stars then as kids are now. When I was about seven or eight years old my hero was Davy Crockett, king of the wild frontier. I just had to have a coonskin cap, just like Davy. So I begged and begged and it paid off and I had my coonskin cap. I wore it EVERYWHERE! There were lots of pictures taken of us kids then and it seems like I'm wearing that coonskin cap in every one of them!

The Indians and Mexican soldiers that I "killed" while wearing it could hardly be counted! Davy would have been proud!

Another movie I play acted about was *Helen of Troy*, a low budget Italian movie about the Trojan Horse. It was the first movie that showed "blood". For weeks I was never caught without my trusty wood slat "sword" and cardboard "shield" and was solely responsible for many "Trojan" deaths!

It's fun now to watch my three year old grandson Teagan being sort of the same way, as he has viewed the "Teenage Mutant Ninja Turtles" movie and has to have his two play swords. Ha!

The downtown *Hollywood Theater* always had Saturday matinee movies for kids in the afternoon and it was always full. There weren't many we missed and went with either friends or cousins. The atmosphere was usually loud and the air was sometimes filled with popcorn or some kind of candy. Jawbreakers hurt when they hit you in the back of your head!

A lot of times when westerns were at the theater, my cousin DuWayne Underthun would get his parents to visit us so he could go to see it. He and I would sometimes walk down to the theater from our house and back again. We saw a number of westerns together. Mom and Dad would only let me walk down there if DuWayne was with me.

About a year later we moved to a new house at 204 S. 12th St. There I went to a different school called Hillcrest and started third grade there. The school grounds were bordered on two sides by Chinhinta Park which was our main hangout when we weren't in school or at home. It had a small creek that ran through it and was probably a scary place had we ever went in there alone. There were vines hanging from trees that we would swing back and forth with over the creek.

There were long hills for sliding on and a small walking bridge that we used to "dam" up with tree branches and stuff so the high school kids couldn't get across. They would holler at us and call us names but they never caught us! The bridge railing was also where I first stuck my tongue on frozen metal! That was stupid! Even now, when I go by there, the memories of those days come flooding back!

It was around this time that I experienced the death of someone close for the first time. My cousin Loren Nagle was eleven when he got sick and died. I was nine years old. He was the only son of my Uncle Earl who was killed in a car accident before I was born.

Loren and I played together occasionally when our families got together for picnics and family get-togethers. Even though Loren's mother remarried, Grampa and Grandma Gilbertson always included him in the events and he was a favorite of theirs. I was about five or six when I first understood that everyone "dies." I remember crying and being very upset about it and Mom and Dad attempting to explain it all to me. Now I saw it firsthand and was rather overwhelmed by it. Being that young, I couldn't really understand that we would never play with or see him again.

His funeral was at Our Savior's Lutheran Church, in Montevideo and I did see him one last time. Again, how does a nine year old understand that someone who looks like they are sleeping but isn't!

My older cousin Delores at the funeral was crying like many others and she had this particular perfume on. To this day, when I smell that perfume, it brings me right back to Loren's funeral. It's strange how something that insignificant can bring back old memories.

The son of our neighbor across the street also died about that time. His name was Steven Vomacka and he had been sick and bedridden at home for quite a while. We used to go over to their house and visit with him, as much as eight year old kids can visit. His funeral was at the Catholic Church in Montevideo and the service was all in Latin which no one understood. Again, death confused me.

Steven's dad, Howard, came over one day raising hell about us kids cutting down some poplar trees he had planted, and Dad was arguing with him about it. We did chop some down because we needed spears! We thought he hated all kids after his son's death, but maybe just us!

There was a "tame" crow in the neighborhood and it would steal items like mittens and small toys left outside. It would carry them up to the house roofs and that's usually the last we saw of them. It probably wasn't tame, it just wasn't real scared!

Halloween was the absolute perfect time to be living in town as there were so many more victims! The only "tricking" we did was soaping a few windows and had heard that the best trick was setting a paper bag of dog poop on someone's front porch and setting fire to it. Then ringing the doorbell before running to hide and watch the homeowners stamping it out and getting poop on their shoes! Only problem was that nobody had dogs in the neighborhood otherwise I'm sure it would have been tried.

At the same time, I was a greedy little brat too as I had figured out a scheme to double my take of candy from the homes in our neighborhood on 12th Street. The Halloween costume Mom and Dad got me that year (I was in 2nd grade) was a Robin Hood outfit with the cocked cap with a feather in it. After I had made all the rounds in that costume and had a pretty good stash of candy, I went home and decided that I didn't have enough so I dug out some old clothes out of boxes put away upstairs and made up another disguise and proceeded to hit up the same houses again. It worked for the most part except for one neighbor who recognized me from earlier and started chewing on me! But was that clever or what?

Chapter 4

Back to the Farm

At the Svor Farm. L to R Ron, Lynn, Nancy and me.

When I was in about the middle of my 3rd grade year, we moved from Montevideo to another farm 11 miles north, three miles east and 1 ½ miles north, and it was about 2 ½ miles from Grandpa and Grandma Gilbertson's farm.

My Dad and my Uncle Curtis' television store had to close down (not my Dad's fault and won't write about it here!) and he had no other recourse but to start farming again. The farm was owned by Glen Flatgard, whose wife (Ruth) and Mom were neighbors by Appleton when they were young.

The farm was 160 acres and we grew corn, soybeans, oats, and sometimes wheat on it. The "farm place" had a ¼ mile driveway to it east from the main road a granary and attached shed, a chicken house, two wood corn cribs, a pig house, barn, and the house. The outhouse was about 100 feet from the house in the grove.

One interesting fact about the chicken house was that many years before we lived there, it served as a rural retail store and post office. There were lots of old items up in the "attic" that had been left over from the store days and me and my brother were told by Dad to stay down from there! Well, that was a sure invitation to explore it when he wasn't around, so we did. We propped up some boards to get up in there and found lots of old style bottles and things we had no clue about. Probably a small fortune in antique items were played with and destroyed by us over the next several years.

Among the items we found was a box of old glass negatives of pictures of old people we didn't know and of a big building being built. We promptly removed the box from the chicken house and it was eventually buried out in the woods where we eventually forgot where, and where today they are still buried! Little did we know that those were probably the only existing pictures of the Mandt Church being rebuilt in 1909 and of the people who built it, including my grandparents. They would be priceless now. We didn't realize this until we were adults and attempted several times to locate them but the grove was big and we just can't remember where they were buried.

The house had been built in the late 1800s and had no running water or bathroom. It was hot in the summer and cold and drafty in the winter. We used to put plastic on the windows and bank around the house with plastic, dirt and straw bales and that helped some.

Three brothers in the apple orchard on the farm.

We all slept upstairs. Mom and Dad in one room, Nancy and I in one bed until she started "changing"! Lynn and Ronnie slept in another room. Nancy got a new single bed and then got her own room, and then I had my own too. In the winter, the glass of water I had on my dresser would sometimes be frozen solid in the morning! The only heat vent upstairs was in my parents' room and it was directly over the oil burner stove downstairs in the living room. It was comfortable sleeping under all the big, heavy quilts though.

When we shared the same bed, Nancy and I would constantly bicker and fight to protect our "side" of the bed. We had this imaginary "line" down the middle which brought instant retaliation if it was crossed! This was a nightly occurrence till we fell asleep. Sometimes I poured water on my chest in bed and blew on it in an attempt to cool off because of the summer heat. We never thought about sleeping downstairs.

Because we had no bathroom, our means of "relieving" ourselves, especially in the winter, was a two gallon white porcelain "pot" that we kept in the "junk room"! It was for both number one and two and since one of my chores was to dump it, accidents did happen if it was near full! After dumping it in the woods or in the outhouse it had to be rinsed out and then a little Hi-Lex bleach put in it. Old habits die hard as, to this day, Mom still keeps the same kind of "pot" upstairs in her house for use if we, or someone else stays overnight with her! I still use it too, much to everyone's disgust, in the middle of the night but only to pee in!

The "junk room" was the correct term for that room. It was where everything not currently used was kept including stuff that never would be used again. Nothing was ever thrown. There were boxes of old toys, junk, old clothes, junk, old furniture, and more junk, along with, of course, "the pot"! We spent a lot of time in there "rummaging" when we were bored in the winter.

Living on a farm, peeing or taking a shit usually happened at the spot we were at the time. The outhouse was used only if we were in the near vicinity! Sometimes we "wiped" sometimes we didn't and lots of underwear were tossed away in the woods if they got too uncomfortable to wear! Corn cobs were usually the "wiper" of choice if they were available and fairly soft from the corn kernels removed by the corn sheller. Tree leaves, grass, weeds, or corn husks also worked but not like a good soft cob!

The outhouse was north of the house and was a two holer! Why there were two holes never really made sense either because I never saw or heard of two people taking a shit together in one of them! That must also have been tradition! The "toilet paper" wasn't real toilet paper, but usually was an old Sears or Montgomery Ward's catalogue. The black and white pages were the best to use because the "colored" pages were more stiff and harder on the butt!

Since I'm still on this subject of relieving one's self, I had thought up a new way of peeing the easy way, without going to the pot or outside, when I was up in my room. I really caught hell from the folks when I was found out but it was very good while it lasted. I had figured out that peeing out my window was really easy to do, it being the right height and this went on most of one summer till I got caught. What gave me away was the metal mesh screen on the window which, after months of being drenched with urine, had started to rust, and that along with yellow pee, had started to run down and stain the white house paint from my window down to the living room window!

Dad finally saw it one day, and figured out real fast what I had been doing. He was pissed! That was the end of that! Dad also believed in the use of corn cobs too, as there were always a few in the tool box on the tractors if he was out in the fields and needed one!

One of us kids' rare attempts at cleaning ourselves, other than the weekly Saturday night bath time was obviously a real fun event. In the summer time during heavy thunderstorms with rain coming down in sheets and no lightning, my brothers and I would strip down and run around the farmyard completely naked and was way better than a bath in previously used bath water. None of us were "mature" then so we had nothing to hide, ha! Dad would also get into the action too and would go behind the garage where he could strip down and stand under the roof edge for a free shower!

About our weekly Saturday night bath which was taken in a large laundry tub. The water was heated on the stove and poured into the tub and Nancy went first. Then me, then Lynn and finally Ronnie. The bath water got progressively dirtier as each one of washed and so Ronnie got the dirtiest water. Even adding water didn't make it any less dirty. That was a week's worth of whatever from me and Lynn. I can't remember if I did but Lynn would threaten to pee in the tub before he got out so Ronnie would have to sit in pee water. Knowing Lynn, I'm pretty sure he did pee in it too. Of course Ronnie would cry and Lynn got hollered at by Mom or Dad.

One thing I always did without fail was "spook patrol" when we came home after dark from shopping in Montevideo, or visiting or any other reason to be gone. As soon as we walked in the house I would inspect each room and the closet downstairs, then up the stairs looking in each room and closet and under each bed and in the "junk" room till I was satisfied there were no spooks or monsters waiting to get me! This went on for years on the farm and I can't remember when I finally quit doing it. I have no idea what I would have done had I found one!

In the winter time us kids still played and did stuff outside almost as much as the other seasons. One indication of that was our continuous raw and scabbed over ears pretty much throughout the coldest months when we got frostbite which the ears were most susceptible to. We really didn't seem to mind ourselves because it just "went with the territory" but the folks were always on us about it and picking at scabs all winter!

There was always blue jeans and cotton long underwear hanging up to dry around the stove. We would come in the house from hours of being outside making snow forts or whatever and our pants, and long underwear and thin cotton gloves would be froze solid! That was what kept us entertained then because the only other things in the house was a television with one channel, or reading books.

As a kid I never gave any thought to what it meant to have a life of living out on a farm and probably never even realized that I loved it so much but just took it for granted.

If I could accurately describe the most contended times about farm life, it would have to be the late afternoons in the springtime. The quiet was only accented by the calls of the meadowlarks, red wing blackbirds, and killdeer out in the pasture. Once in a while a cow would "moo", and pigs would "grunt" but otherwise it was pure quiet and contentment. To me, it was "heaven" compared to living in Montevideo.

I always had more friends there in town to do things with but it couldn't compare to the peace and quiet of farm life. The scents of the new growth of grass in the pasture, the new crops coming up and alfalfa fields and yes, even the manure pile smelled good to us, as cow, pig and chicken shit smells totally different on a small farm, than the big "factory" feed barns do now.

Part of my daily chores was shoveling shit out of the barn gutters and dumping it in the manure pile outside the back door. And about once a year our neighbor Ernest Johnson, would hire me to come over and shovel out his pig house, which took a couple days. He paid me $5.00 a day so that was good money then! I would fork it in a manure spreader and then he would spread it on his fields. Pig shit was a lot worse than cow shit and when I got home at the end of the day, I had to take my shit covered clothes off outside before Mom would let me in the house.

Country School

The country school we went to was called District 64, later changed to District 311, and was ¼ mile southeast of our farm place. It was a typical one room building with an entryway, closet areas on both sides where we hung coats and stacked our lunch pails, and a small toilet on each side past the closets. Off the main room there was a small library, and a full basement underneath.

We started there in the middle of my third grade year and out of about 30 kids from first to sixth grade, I only knew my cousin Gary

Armstrong. The teacher was Mrs. Irma Paul and she drove there every day from Louisburg, MN, about an hour away.

Going to the bathroom was, again, "the traditional" one finger/two finger signal. There was an outhouse too but it was used only during recess or to play Annie-I-over with. One time during a school play one of the Christianson boys was at the front doing a skit or reading when all of a sudden he stopped and raised his hand with one finger up. The school was full of kids and parents too.

Well, no one said anything and they couldn't figure out what he was doing. He was just waiting for permission to go pee, like during school, but didn't get any so finally he lowered his arm, slapped the side of his leg and said "too late"! Then this wet spot on his pants started getting bigger and pee started to run on the floor! It was pretty embarrassing for him and I'm just glad it wasn't me!

School plays were a very big deal to the kids and we really looked forward to the Christmas play. Everyone got to participate in something, be it skits or saying pieces or singing. The parents all sat at our desks and on folding chairs. We had a "curtain" that we opened and closed the skits with. Afterwards there was a potluck lunch and bags of peanuts and Christmas candy for us kids.

Another annual event was "shot day". This was where we all got to go to another school, along with the other area county schools and get the Tuberculosis test. This was done by an injection of serum under the skin of our inside forearm to test for the disease. Of course we all dreaded that day and tried to get out of it, but to no avail. We had to stand in line for it and the closer we got to the needle the whiter our faces got!

We all managed to survive it and it really didn't even hurt, but every year the two girls, Diane and Arlene, would pee their pants in the line and sometimes faint! We always had great fun over that! Again, glad it wasn't me! These girls ate boogers in school too so we didn't have much sympathy for them!

A year or two later tragedy struck the Randt family when their only boy Steven was run over by a tractor his dad was driving and was killed. He was probably in 2nd grade at the time. It was a real blow to a small close knit community and I remember everyone going to the funeral in Clara City. His dad, Fred Randt, was never the same after that!

My classmates were Joey Lynne, Rachel Laeger and Jerry Christianson, who were also my classmates when we graduated from high school. We still see each other occasionally at class reunions or around Montevideo.

Recess was, of course, the best part of school and the same games were played there too. Some of our activities during recess got us into trouble with the teacher too, like throwing snowballs, bringing frogs or snakes into school, wrapping snakes around the girls' necks, or putting them in the teacher's desk! She *really* frowned on those pranks!

Our favorite game during the spring months of school was softball and our school was particularly good at it as we played against the other schools and routinely beat them. The other schools being Districts 66, 33, and 54. It was always a game I excelled at, especially pitching.

During my sixth grade year the teacher decided we should have a team captain and that we were to have an election between me and Joey Lynne, as we were the best players. One of the tasks as a teacher was to instill in us a sense of fair play and to be courteous and respectful to those against whom we compete! On the day of the election, I obviously forgot all that and since I wanted to be the captain so bad, when the ballots were passed out to write the name on, I voted for myself and not Joey as fair play dictated! She made that known before we voted too.

When the votes were counted I had won with all 100% of the votes! Even Joey had voted for me! I should have politely voted for him but never realized no one else would either. Another embarrassing moment! Mrs. Paul was not happy with me voting for me. We all got over it thought and went on to more victories. Ha!

The small school library was my second favorite part of school, next to recess, and I was a voracious book reader. I'm sure I read almost all of the books in there and some more than once. I had very good grades in country school but they changed for the worse when I started high school, mainly due in large part to the huge amounts of new books in the big library! Reading always was a priority!

In the summer months of school vacation, the country bookmobile would stop at our school or an hour or so once a week. This was a large van full of book shelves and books and every week I would bring home anywhere from 5-10 books and have them all read in time for the next bookmobile visit.

Among the books I checked out once was the book "The Great Sioux Uprising of 1862." I had been reading it outside one day and apparently set it on the trunk of our car and forgot about it. We went someplace later that day and the book fell off, never to be found, though we retraced our tracks looking for it. The folks got a bill from the County for it for around $5 dollars, and were not happy with me!

The first time Mom & Dad took me to the City Library in Montevideo, I thought I had "died and gone to heaven"! Having been only in small country school libraries with only a hundred or so books, I never thought that there could be so many more than those and was in awe when walking through the library doors for the first time. Many thousands lined the four walls and I wasted no time in grabbing a stack of books I had never seen before! This was before I had seen a bookmobile so what a treat it was not having to reread a book just for something to read. After going to bed, I remember sneaking a flashlight in my room and laying under the covers and reading most nights until falling asleep.

Our Cows

Me, Lynn, Nancy and Ronnie on the fence between the barn and the pig house.

We had twelve milk cows and they were milked by hand until Dad got a milking machine setup that was powered by compressed air. That was a real work saver. We would wash dirt or shit off the cow's teats, hook the pail on a strap over the cows back and just slide the rubber "suckers" over each teat and let air do the work. After the cow was milked, the collector pail was then poured into a large milk can and then stored in the milk cooler until the milk truck picked it up once or twice a week. At times in the winter when our driveway was drifted over, we had to load the milk cans on sleds and pull them a quarter mile to the end of our driveway for the milk truck to pick up.

When it was milking time, in the summer months when the cattle were out in the pasture, Dad would "call" them from the barn by hollering "Come boss, come boss" several times real loud and up to the barn they would come! That was something they would never do for me, as I tried quite often but they wouldn't obey my pre-pubescent high pitched voice! Only Dad could do it. Once in a while there would be a straggler or two and we would run out after it and chase it up to the barn.

There were 12 stanchions in the barn for the cattle which were metal and wood mechanical neck locks that we would slide closed after the cattle put their heads through. There was lots of room in them, as the cattle could even lay down. They just couldn't pull their heads out.

The cows all had their own particular stanchion too as they would almost line up in order when they came in the barn. Once in a while two would try to occupy the same stanchion, and had to be helped to their right place as we knew where they were supposed to be also. I'm sure that came from them being in the same spot through the winter when they were in the barn all the time till warmer weather came.

The cows all had names but to this day I can only remember one. "Prune ball". I'm sure the rest were pretty odd names too as us kids named them.

We had to try our hand at "riding" the cows too but that was mainly just sitting on them when they were locked in their stanchions. Their backbones stuck out so much that it really hurt to be on them very long. I got up on one occasionally out in the barnyard but would promptly get bucked off and that's when the backbone really hurt!

When I was around eleven old, Dad got a hernia and had to have it operated on so he called my cousin David Olson over to do the milking while he was laid up and he stayed with us for about two weeks. It was great fun getting to hang out with an older cousin. He was about 17 or 18 at the time and when we didn't have chores to do and milking was done, we would go hunting in the woods for crows and animals. We found several baby crows one day that must have been trying to fly and were just sitting on branches by the ground. We promptly killed them with tree branches, as crows were nasty birds! We thought nothing of it.

David bought me my first hunting knife one day when we went to the Coast-to-Coast hardware store in Montevideo. It had a red handle and a leather sheath and was I ever proud of it. I still have it to this day. My older cousins were really cool!

One of the things that was great about our old barn was how cozy it became in the winter. Since the cattle were in there through the winter months, and though not heated except by them, it was still comfortable in there and thick with steam from all the cows' breath and the warmth of their large bodies.

Lots of times I would crawl in by a cow that was laying down and sit leaning against the side of the cow. They didn't seem to mind it either and it was very comfortable with the heat from the cow through the winter clothes. Not all of them would let me do that, but a few would.

When I was down in the dumps about school stuff or something I got in trouble over, just going in the barn and spending time with the cattle always seemed to make things alright again.

After several more years of milking, Dad sold most of the cattle and kept only two for the family drinking milk. That was then a part of my chores to do when I got home from school. He also sold the milking machine equipment so then we did the milking by hand. It was a pretty simple task to do but was very tiring to the hand and fingers.

The first thing to learn was to hold the teat in your hand, squeeze the thumb and forefinger together first and then to squeeze the other three fingers in descending order to force the milk out and into the pail. It usually took around ½ hour or so to milk two to three gallons. Sometimes the cow would kick me if I was "handling" it wrong! No major injuries though.

One time I was milking in the winter time and had learned from watching Dad that I could squirt milk at the cats and they would stand up on their hind legs and claw at the milk stream and drink it while I squirted it. The cats were behind the cow and on the other side of the manure gutter. I was squirting milk at one of the cats, Fluffy, while sitting on the milk stool with an almost full pail of milk, when the milk stream started diminishing and getting weaker and the cat followed it down and finally fell forward on one of the cow's rear legs.

When the cat grabbed the leg it obviously did so with its claws extended, and the next thing I know, I was laying on my back in the gutter full of shit and covered in what the milk pail was holding! The cow had kicked so hard and fast that I couldn't figure out at first how I got there! I was covered with shit on my whole back, milk all over the front of me and had to explain to Mom and Dad why we wouldn't have milk that day. They were pissed! Another lesson learned there! To top it all off, the temperature was well below zero and by the time I got to the house the shit and milk had frozen solid on me.

When we first got our cows, they all had horns so not long after that we dehorned them. I'm not sure of the real reason to do that but probably because they were somewhat dangerous and it was harder getting them in the stanchions. Some uncles and neighbors came over to help. Dad had borrowed a dehorner tool and each cow was tied up so it couldn't jump around, and then each horn was popped off leaving a deep socket. Right away blood started shooting out in little "jets" and sprayed all over!

My uncle Lowell had collected large amount of cob webs from the barn and this was then applied to each horn socket to stop the bleeding. It probably helped heal too. I never realized that cobwebs had a purpose! Basically cobwebs were just spider webs full of barn dust.

Occasionally I had to help Dad to birth a calf when the cow was having a hard time pushing it out. We did this by tying baling twine around the calf's front legs while the calf was still in the womb and then pulling on it when the mother cow would have a contraction. It worked every time as we never lost a calf.

Note: For those who have never stepped in a fresh hot cow pie barefooted and squeezed the steaming hot shit through their toes, they will never know what they missed. Pure pleasure and an incredible experience!

Our Pigs

We also raised pigs and more often than not, they were a great form of entertainment for us kids. They were always easy targets for whatever we were holding or could pick up, including a BB gun, and they were a lot easier to ride than cattle!

We learned to sneak up from behind them, then jump and straddle their back and clamp our legs as tight as we could as there was nothing else to hold onto. What a ride! Some would run in a fairly straight line. Others would run and turn in circles, and some would start chasing us when we fell off, so we learned that we better hit the ground running! We never got bit but had some close calls.

Dad would really raise hell with us if he knew we were riding them too, as pigs can't sweat and it was really hard on them during the hot summer time. I don't think any of them died from it though. Again, that was something we only did when Dad wasn't around.

I used to be particularly mean at times to them and it seems they always kept an eye on me when I was around the barnyard. When bored, I would shoot at them with my BB gun and it was great fun to shoot at the boar pig's "scrotum" when they were on top of a sow making little pigs! I admit that was very cruel on my part! But Lynn and Ronnie did it too! Boy, did they squeal!

When the sows were having their litters of little ones, Dad would pen them up separate to keep the baby pigs safe from the other pigs. He would pen up 5 or 6 in the other half of the barn, across from the cattle with an isle between them and the cattle.

Well, the sows knew me well and when I went in the barn it would get very quiet while they would watch me like a hawk! One of my favorite things to do was to spit on them and my goal was to hit them between the eyes with the spit. This really pissed them off! The doors on our barn were split doors, with a top and bottom we could close or keep open. Lucky for me that the top of the door behind the cows, going out to the barnyard was open one day, as I was making my rounds of the penned up sows and spitting on them. This one huge sow (approximately 500 lbs. or more) just couldn't take the disrespect any longer and went after me!

She jumped over most of the pen boards, which were about 3 feet high, broke through the rest and it was a race for survival for me! She chased me up the isle in front of the cows, then around the end, and down behind the cows to the barn door and since the top was open I was in full stride and dove headfirst through the door and out in the yard. Of course right out the door was the manure pile so I was again covered in shit. At least the sow stopped at the door. I don't know what would have happened if the door had been closed, as the sow was right on my heels! Dad wasn't around either. I can't remember how I explained it to him but he was pissed! That was the end of the spitting on the pigs.

When the little pigs were three -four months old they were given shots to prevent various diseases and the males were castrated. Some of my uncles and neighbors would come over and help do it as it cost too much to have the veterinarian do it. Dad learned how to give shots and I would help hold up the pigs by the front legs and their head in between as Dad would give them shots under their legs around the armpit area.

The pigs didn't care for that at all and once in a while I would get "nipped" on the fingers. I never did help castrating though. Just help catch them. The men would lay them on their back, pinch off the "nuts" and remove them with a razor blade. Then the wound would be doused with kerosene and off they ran squealing. They didn't move around much for several days, but then they were okay!

We raised the pigs for market and when they reached a certain size would be sold. It was always kind of a "circus" atmosphere when the truck came, the loading chute was down, and the attempt to load the pigs was started! Dad never had much patience when it came to livestock "misbehaving" and he would be hollering and cussing with an electric prod in one hand and a stick in the other trying to force pigs into something they never saw before. It was pretty exciting! Finally it was done and America was fed! Most kids learn most of the "swear" words from their friends. I think we learned ours from Dad! Ha!

Pigs were also meat eaters too, as piles of chicken feathers in the pig house every once in a while would attest.

When we had the dairy herd, several times a cow would develop mastitis, and have to be put down, as there was no cure for it. It affected their milk somehow and was detected by dark little lumps in the milk. Dad called the "rendering" truck once to pick up a dead cow. (This truck had a big bin on the back for holding dead farm animals and stunk so bad we could almost smell it coming down the road.)

The next time he had to shoot one, he hooked up the tractor to it with a log chain and then dragged it out on the far side of the barnyard, cut it open and the pigs took over from there. In a couple weeks or so the only thing left were the bones that ended up scattered all over the place.

We also fed carp to them too after a fishing trip over to the Churchill Dam by Watson. Some of those carp would weigh ten pounds or more and we wouldn't eat them but the pigs sure liked them. Pure protein!

Butchering day was always a day we looked forward to. Grandpa and Grandma Gilbertson, my Aunt and Uncle Mildred and Lowell Armstrong and my Uncle Lyle Gilbertson would come over with various pots and knives and meat saws, everyone having a job to do.

The prospective pig would be separated from the others out in the barnyard then Dad or one of my uncles would shoot it in the head with the .22 caliber rifle. It would then be dragged over to a tree to be hung up by the back feet. The throat would then be cut to collect the blood for making blood sausage, and then it would be disemboweled. A large amount of water was boiled and this was poured over the carcass to soften the hair and make it easier to scrape off.

Us kids, being sick of mind at times, would take great pleasure in playing with the pig entrails. The stomach, being bloated up with air and other stuff was fun to jump up and down on until it finally broke! God only knows what we did with some of the other "items"! It all eventually disappeared.

We let the carcass hang till the next day, when the actual butchering began. My Aunt Mildred made the blood sausage, which was better than anyone else made. It was one of my favorite meals! Everything else was cut up, packaged and marked and put in the deep freeze. The extra fat was rendered down (fried) for cooking fat and resulted in piles of cracklins that we ate up fast. They also boiled the head down to make head cheese but that's one thing I wouldn't eat!

Chores

Since I was the oldest boy I was deemed responsible enough to complete numerous daily chores around the farm.

Since we also had a wood and coal burning stove in the kitchen, a near daily ritual when getting home from school in the winter months was for Dad and I to go out in the grove and find a dead ash tree to cut up for firewood using a two-man buck saw. My first ever chores included feeding and watering the chickens, putting down straw bedding for the nests and then the dreaded job of cleaning out the chicken crap. In fact, almost all my chores involved shoveling shit!

I didn't so much mind the chores I had to do in the barn though. When the milk cows had calves, I would mix up milk replacer in pails with a nipple on it about the size of a cow's teat and feed them a couple times a day.

For the milk cows, if it was winter they stayed in their stantions continuously and I would have to carry in bales of hay for them, and silage, and carry in five gallon pails of water for each one at a time and also pour out a portion of either ground corn or ear corn for them to eat. This also was a couple times a day, early morning or late afternoon after school. I didn't have to do much for them in the summertime as they were then only in the barn to be milked.

I had to clean out the gutters which, in the winter, when the cows were in the barn 24/7, were always in need of cleaning. We used a six tined fork for most of it which would be carried to the back door and pitched onto the manure pile but then had to use a grain scoop shovel for the cow piss and that always was a challenge to get a scoop full out the door without tipping it!

A couple times a month I would help Dad grind up ear corn with a grinder powered by the power takeoff on the tractor and this would feed cattle, pigs and chickens. During the winter months, we burned wood in the heat stove in the kitchen so almost every day after I got home from school, Dad and I would head to the woods with the two man buck saw and saw up firewood and carry back to the house. Then I got to carry the "pot" outside to dump! Ha!

Our Chickens

Most farms back then had chickens and ours was no exception. They provided us with eggs, meat, and sometimes entertainment! They were always an easy target for sticks or rocks or corncobs (remember those?) and even for arrows. Of course we didn't want to kill the chickens so when my brothers or I would shoot arrows at them, we would shove a corncob chunk on the end of the arrow so then it would bounce off the chicken.

Once in a while though, the arrow pushed through the corncob and impaled the chicken! There would be a chicken laying on its side with an arrow through it and legs and wings flapping till it finally died or we put it out of its misery! Since we had so many, those weren't noticed and we never got caught. It was just chalked up to the natural mortality rate of dumb chickens!

Picking eggs was part of my chores and one I hated the most. We had this "laying" compartment in the chicken house where they laid the eggs. The top flipped up on hinges for us to get at the eggs and if some were still "laying" we reached under the chicken for the eggs. And heaven help the chickens that pecked then, because that was another excuse to nail the chicken with a fist or something. I guess we were a little mean to them!

The eggs we collected were brought to the house where we put them in a pail full of water and a cleaning solution and this was put on an electric contraption that "twisted" the pail back and forth for a certain amount of time and which cleaned the eggs by motion and abrasion. We then crated up the eggs in special boxes and they were taken in to Montevideo on Friday evenings to be sold before we went shopping.

We also butchered chickens for meat and this was done quite often. At first I just helped Dad by holding the legs and Dad the head when he chopped it off with an axe. And then they would be dunked in boiling water to loosen the feathers for plucking, and that was also my job. Before all this happened though, we had to catch them and we did this with a long steel rod with a hook on the end that would hook around a chicken's leg. This was also a challenge as we had to trap them somehow as they were faster than us.

After I was a little older and bigger, it became my job to catch, kill, pluck, and clean them. Since I still wasn't strong enough to hold down a chicken with one hand and chop the head off with the axe in the other, I had to resort to trickery to do it!

I had learned from Uncle Lyle that a chicken could be put to sleep by catching it, folding its head under a wing and turning it around in large circles out front of me for a couple minutes. It really did work! I would then quickly lay the chicken down on the chopping stump, pull its head out and stretch it out and then grab the axe with two hands and chop the head off before it woke up! Immediately the headless chicken was off and running and squirting blood around till it finally collapsed.

I had to be quick in killing it after I pulled its head out because that "sleep" didn't last long! Once in a while one would get away if I was too slow with the axe.

Fried and roasted chicken was always one of our favorite meals and we would usually bicker over who got the gizzard. Ha!

In the fall it was time to round up the chickens and get them into the chicken house to survive the winter. We would stretch out lath fencing V shaped from the front door and then head out to the far side of the grove to start "herding" them. Since they were all over the farm place we missed a lot of them on the initial drive and would then have to catch them one by one with the "chicken catcher hook" over the next several weeks.

Farming

Threshing day at our farm. The wagon would be filled with oats.

We farmed 160 acres with four different crops and used the "rotation" method of not growing the same crop on the same field two years in a row. We started out with one older Minneapolis Moline tractor and that's what Dad taught me to drive. He then bought another newer model a year or two later when he decided that I could do some of the fieldwork on my own. I started out by driving grain wagons and hay trailers and then dragging fields before planting, and then on to cultivating corn & beans.

I hated plowing because our tractors could only pull a 3 bottom blow and it took several weeks of long days to get the fields plowed. When we plowed up alfalfa fields, which had very thick root systems, we hooked both of our tractors together with a log chain to pull the plow. After lots of yelling and hand signals by Dad we finally became a "team" and it went smoother after that. I drove the front tractor and Dad the rear one so he could operate the plow levers.

One time, on the southeast field, we were plowing together when I saw a baby rabbit trying to run down the plow furrow in front of my tractor. Since the tractor tire ran in the furrow and it was too deep for the rabbit to crawl out, I knew it would be run over if we didn't stop. I hollered at dad that we need to stop (both tractors had to stop together or a motor could be damaged) but he kept shaking his head cause it was hard to get started again. Well, sure enough, the tractor wheel finally caught up to and ran over the little rabbit. I felt terrible about it but dad had a point!

After a field was plowed under, it had to be dragged before planting. The drag was about 16 to 20 feet wide and had downward pointing teeth that dug into the dirt and smoothed it out better before running the grain planter over it. I liked dragging because it wasn't very heavy and the tractor could go faster.

One time, when Mom & Dad were gone for a day and I was told to have the northwest field dragged, I came up with the bright idea of using our old '51 Ford in place of the tractor. I figured that since a car can go lots faster than a tractor, I could get it all done in a fraction of the time and then spend the rest of the day with my cousin Gary Armstrong.

Never mind that I never saw anyone else ever use a car for that and the fact that I didn't understand gearing and axle ratios! So after the folks left, I unhooked the tractor from the drag out in the field, drove home, and got the Ford started and got it hooked up to the drag somehow. I really thought I was so smart to think of this and proceeded to start the car, put it in gear, and let the clutch out. It died!

Try as I could, I couldn't get it to budge an inch. Had I understood gearing I wouldn't have even attempted it, so another great idea shot to hell! That effort wasted about two hours so had to spend even more of the day out there. Lesson learned. I could picture myself in the car dragging the field at high speed in front of a huge cloud of dust too! What a huge letdown.

After the dragging was done, Dad did all the planting so I was off the hook for fieldwork for a month or so. Once the corn & beans were a certain height then the cultivating started. At first Dad did all that too but later he taught me after he thought I could handle the tractor well enough.

We had a four row cultivator and it required a lot of concentration because if I got off track even a little I would dig up 4 rows of future crops, not just one! Every once in a while I would have a "brain fart" and dig up a few yards of crop and it would really show up during harvest. I got an ass chewing more than once from Dad, ha!

Another one of the summer field jobs was cutting the corn out of the bean field. Because of crop rotation beans were usually planted in the field the corn was the previous year and so any corn left in the field would grow the following year. This caused problems with the bean yield as it was tested at the elevator and if there is too much corn or weed seeds in the bean sample we would be docked in price for it.

So every summer we would each have a weed cutter or scythe and walk the bean rows and cut out the offending plants. Not a fun job when it's hot out but the field sure looked nice afterward. It still bothers me now when I drive by bean fields that have corn and weeds all over them. I just want to get out there and start cutting weeds.

When we had the dairy herd we also had a field of alfalfa that we cut and baled several times a year for hay for them. This entailed cutting it with a mower behind the tractor, letting it dry for a week or two, raking it into rows, and then baling it and stacking it by the barn.

Since we didn't have a baling machine we usually hired Harry Swenson to do it. He lived with his brother Martin on a farm place across the road from my Uncle Lyle and that's all he did for a living. He also was apparently allergic to soap as any exposed skin was almost completely a black/brown/gray color! I think the only time he washed his face and hands were when he baled our hay, as Mom wouldn't let him in the house for lunch or dinner if he didn't wash first! He didn't like it but he was hungry!

Years later, after Harry died, his brother went out to the shed by the house, got a rope, and hung himself. What a sad occasion.

Besides being good for the cattle, hay bales were good for my brother and I too cause we would make "forts" with them to hide and play in. We even made 2 story ones sometimes and stacked them to make long tunnels.

Baling was quite labor intensive as it had to be stacked on the trailer behind the baler and then brought to the barn to be restacked. Since each hay bale weighed from 50 to 75 pounds or more I was too young and small to stack them at first so my job was to hook them with a bale hook as they were coming up out of the baler, and slide them back to Dad to stack them. Later, when I was older and stronger, I could do more of the heavy lifting and would hire out to the neighbors for around $5.00 a day to help them bale hay or straw.

One of our neighbors I especially hated to work for was Hilmer Nelson. He was a big man and liked his bales heavy and when he called to see if I was available to help I tried to get out of it but Dad usually made me go! He had his baler made heavier than anyone else and for me they were almost too much! I knew he didn't think my work was worth paying for but there were no other boys around other than my cousin Gary.

An event I looked forward to was threshing oats in the late summer. It didn't happen every summer but when it did it was a very fun time. Grandpa Gilbertson was usually in charge of the operation since he had the threshing machine. Even when I was a young kid threshing wasn't done much anymore because of the big combines that were more efficient, but it was done more for nostalgia purposes.

Threshing involved cutting the oats with a swathing machine (binder) which would bind sheaves of oats into bundles, which would then be stacked together, probably four to six bundles per stack and they would be left to dry standing upright somewhat like a small teepee.

Come threshing day the threshing machine would be set up and would be powered by a long belt turned by the power take off wheel from the tractor to the wheel on the threshing machine. Several wagons would be there to hold the oats and several hay wagons to collect the bundles from the field.

Since I was the oldest kid, it was my job to drive the tractor and hay wagon to pick up the bundles from the field. There were a couple men that walked along side of the wagon and would fork the bundles onto the wagon. When it was full I would drive it back to the threshing machine and the bundles would be fed into one end. Inside, the machine would thresh up the bundles, separating the oats from the straw, the oats being channeled up an auger to the wagon and the straw being shot out a funnel adding to a large straw pile. This straw was used for bedding for the cattle and pigs. At Grandpa's farm, he had built a "barn" which was a series of posts and boards and chicken wire that he fashioned rooms out of. Then straw was threshed over it in a huge pile and then underneath was the new "cattle barn". It was a real cozy place too!

Grandpa was the caretaker of the threshing machine and he was constantly walking around and climbing on it while it was operating, with an oil can or grease gun making adjustments here & there. He had used one for most of his life and probably knew more about it than anyone else. That same threshing machine still rests in the grove south of the barn on their farm where my Uncle Lyle still lives. It still looks like it could work again with some reconditioning.

The tractor Grandpa Gilbertson had was an old Model B John Deere that he got when Dad was young. It was started by turning a large hand wheel on the side of the engine by hand. Something I could never do when I was younger, but I sure drove it a lot. My uncle Verdie Gilbertson now has rescued the tractor in the woods behind the shed and has restored it to "new" condition. I kept an article about it from the Montevideo American Newspaper. Someday it will passed down to someone in the family

Threshing day was also a gathering together of the families of all who helped out. It was mostly my Uncles and Aunts and Grandpa and Grandma Gilbertson, but also a few neighbors. Everyone brought various kinds of food so the lunches & dinners were great!

In the fall the soybeans and corn were harvested and we used the "communal" combine for the soybeans. I believe it actually belonged to Uncle Lyle. I didn't know of any farmer out by us who owned all the machinery required for farming. What we didn't store in the granary, we usually sold at the Big Bend elevator about five miles west. I got to drive there on occasion with the tractor and a load of grain in the wagon to sell. It took about an hour or so one way as the tractor wasn't very fast.

We only had a "one row" corn picker that was pulled by the tractor so we had to have a neighbor with an "attached" corn picker on the front & sides of the tractor to "open up" the corn field so we could drive our tractor over the picked rows and not knock down any standing corn rows. It took us several days of steady picking to finish the corn fields. The machinery that farmers use now could do it in several hours!

Farming had its many hazards and dangers too. Mom's neighbor by Appleton, Marshall Gjengdahl, was killed out in a field when the seat of his tractor broke off and he fell backwards on a field tiller, hit his head and was caught up in the tiller. The tractor kept on going around in circles till a neighbor noticed it and got it stopped. This happened when I was a teenager and we visited with them on occasion so I knew him pretty well.

The real danger situation I was involved in was actually caused by me and I was around 14-15 years old at the time. I was out in the west field one morning, plowing when I decided to smoke a cigarette! I had started smoking with my cousin a year or so earlier and usually smoked several a day, in hiding of course! Anyway, Dad wasn't home that morning so I wasn't worried about being seen. I had a cigarette lighter but couldn't get it lit as it was out of lighter fluid. As it had become a habit to me, I panicked a little and tried and tried to get it to light. No go!

Finally an idea came to mind that I had a whole tank of gas in the tractor which I figured was about the same as lighter fluid. I took the lighter apart and attempted to dip it in the tank but I couldn't quite reach the gasoline and was worried that I might drop it down in the tank. So that wasn't going to work either. I then decided to check out the tool box to see if anything in there would work. There just so happened to be a length of baling twine in there and another idea hit me! I could dangle the twine in the gas tank and drip it on my lighter!

I climbed up on top of the gas tank and straddled it in front of the gas cap. I got my lighter ready, cigarette in mouth and dipped the twine in, soaked it with gas, pulled it out and started dripping it on the lighter wick. That's when real stupidity struck! I then decided to light my cigarette before I put the gas cap back on, so I flicked the wheel on the lighter, the flint sparked, and 'WOOSH', the fumes coming from the open gas tank ignited. The tank held about 25 gallons of gas and had been filled that morning, which saved my life. If the tank had been nearer to empty the tank would have blown up.

Now I'm straddling the tank with the burning fumes shooting up before me with a low roaring sound and I'm scared shitless not knowing if I should jump off and run or what. I guess for some reason I'll never know, I sat there and slammed my open palm over the opening and that smothered the flames! I sat there for a while and thought about what had transpired, got off the tank, turned off the engine, and walked back to the house and up to my room and went to bed, shaking so bad I couldn't even talk.

Dad came home in the afternoon and I was still in bed shaking! He saw the tractor sitting out in the field and thought something had broken down. I finally managed to tell him I got real sick out there and he bought it! I eventually told him what really happened years later and he just shook his head.

Several years later, I was about 17 years old at the time, Dad and I were out combining beans in the northeast field and I was standing on the combine and grabbing the tall pig weeds after the sickle bar cut them off and before they went through the combine. The weed stalks were dry and rough so I was wearing gloves to protect my hands. Something a person should never do around moving machinery parts. Well, sure enough, I grabbed a big weed right by the pulley that turns the combine swather wheel and my glove caught between the pulley wheel and the belt and it pulled my left hand in by my pointer finger! Luckily it wasn't a drive belt and pulley or I would have probably lost my hand, or more.

I started screaming at Dad and he stopped everything and jumped off and tried to turn the pulley back but it wouldn't budge, and I'm hollering and swearing and couldn't feel my finger and thought it had been cut off! Dad finally got his knife out and cut the new belt and finally pulled my finger out. The pressure had almost completely flattened it and it was bleeding and really started to hurt bad once the blood started flowing through it. He said we had to get to the doctor and to get on the tractor but I was about ready to pass out so I said I would walk or run alongside instead.

When we got up to the house it looked a little better and we washed it off and soaked it in ice water and never did see a doctor. I had no feeling in it on the inside half of the finger for almost 2 years, even after going in the Air Force. The weird thing was when I held a cigarette between the 2 fingers. It felt like the cigarette was balancing on the middle finger!

Dad had just put a new belt on the combine too before harvest time and he wasn't happy about having to buy another one as they were quite expensive.

In the summertime when I wasn't in school, one of my responsibilities was to take lunch out in the field to Dad midmorning and midafternoon. It was usually a sandwich, cookies or cake and Kool- aid and coffee. I would meet him at the end of a corn or bean row and he would turn the tractor so a wheel provided shade and we would sit there eating and talking small talk! Bonding time I guess. I really enjoyed that unless I was in trouble! Ha!

In the springtime and after the snow had melted one of my favorite things to do was put on five buckle overshoes and make rivers of water in the plowed fields. It was rather addicting and fun to get the biggest water flow from the low spots and channel smaller rivers into bigger ones. Dad sure didn't like it though and would chew on me for doing it. He wanted the melt off to absorb naturally into the soil as he knew the value of sub soil moisture. Nowadays with tiling of farm land water can't seemed to be drained off fast enough.

Our Cats

The summer after moving back to the farm, we got our first cats. My Uncle Gordon brought us two cats from his farm by Bellingham. He had caught them and put them in a gunny sack and when he let them out at our place they ran and hid and we never saw them for several days. When they finally showed themselves they wouldn't come near us and would only eat and drink the food and milk we put out for them when we weren't around.

One was a brownish long haired angora that we named "Fluffy" and the other was a short-haired gray and white cat we eventually called "Mother Cat". Fluffy was also female and these two were the start of our "cat dynasty"!

They both were pretty wild and I remember spending hours sitting in the northwest barn door with a bowl of milk and table scraps trying to coax them to eat. They would get closer and closer and usually would run off again if I moved at all. Finally they would get up close enough to eat and watch me at the same time and finally decided I wasn't going to hurt them. It took longer yet before they would let me pet them while they ate, but once I was able to do that, then we became friends. It wasn't long after that that male cats came around and not long after that, we had our first litters of kittens!

We had lots of fun playing with them once they got "eyes", and that was also the "safe" time of their lives! Dad quickly figured that we would soon be overrun by cats if we didn't have "crowd control", so when he found the litters of kittens before their eyes had opened he would kill them by "thumping" them against a wall. I guess it was a harsh way of it but not as cruel as some who would drown them.

He was still soft-hearted and couldn't kill them once their eyes were open. I think he enjoyed playing with them as much as we did. My brothers and I would try to hide the new litters from Dad too so he wouldn't find them but on many of the occasions the mother would carry them right back to the first nest, and sometimes to their deaths!

Our cat population eventually peaked at 33 adult cats and when my Uncle Donald visited one time he made up a big sign and put it up down by our mailbox which stated that we had "33 cats for sale, cheap!" Mom was so embarrassed! We still all laugh about it 40 years later!

Every cat had a name and some were obvious descriptive names and others were corny and senseless! One of our favorites was "Orangie" and another we named "Korticks". Orangie was, of course, orange and Korticks was white, black and some orange and tan. There were many other cats and names through the years there but these are the ones I remember. Both of them were offspring of "Fluffy", which was, of course, fluffy!

Food for the cats was always an issue also because of their number. Mom would put out a big bowl of table scraps for the dog and cats and that was always a circus affair! The dog would eat first and would bite any cat that got in her way. The cats would attempt to sneak in and grab a bite while the dog was distracted but in the end most of them got something to eat.

The female cats would go out in the field or woods and catch various critters and usually carry them back where the tomcats or younger cats would steal them away. Feeding the cats was also a good reason for me to kill as many birds as I could with my BB gun!

Because the cats were fed off of the side porch, they usually hung out there most of the time waiting for food, and this pissed Dad off in a big way! He was constantly kicking cats off the porch and swearing at them and they would be flying through the air and screeching and running off to hide, for a while till Dad left and then they would all be back up there again. It was fun to watch! This went on every day.

None of the cats were "inside" cats and one time when Mom and Dad were gone someplace, we brought one of the adult cats in the house. Big mistake, as it had never been in there before and all of a sudden it panicked and started running around the house and trying to jump out the windows and bouncing off the glass! We finally grabbed a bed sheet and trapped it and got it back outside! Orangie got used to coming in the house eventually and that also led to a rather exciting incident, at least for us kids!

We all were going into Montevideo one day for grocery shopping & other things. Mom had taken out a pound of butter from the deep freeze to throw on a plate on the kitchen table while we were gone and didn't notice that when she was leaving the house Orangie slipped in the door behind her! Well, we got back home several hours later and when we went in the house Mom noticed that the plate she thought she put butter on was completely clean! She thought that she must have forgot to take the butter out and then went to the closet in the back of the house to put her coat away and get butter out of the deep freeze.

Out of the closet ran the cat with this terrible odor following it! All over the bottom of the closet was splattered approximately 1 pound of butter that the cat had eaten off the plate on the table and then licked it clean! Buttery diarrhea was on or in most of the shoes and Mom was pissed! Of course us kids thought it was pretty funny and tried to picture a hungry cat attempting to gulp down that much butter!

I had notoriously bad athlete's foot as a young pre-teen and one day my youngest brother Ronnie was on the porch playing with something while I had just came to the house and was taking my shoes off. Of course my feet smelled real bad and at an opportune moment I stuck my foot in Ronnie's face and my big toe went in his mouth!

Immediately he started puking on the porch and the cats started swarming over the puke and fighting over it and I'm laughing about it and Ronnie's crying about it and the cats are screeching about it and here comes Mom to see what the commotion was! Needless to say, I got a few good swats on the butt for that little trick!

I will use that event to explain the difference of the 3 Norwegian terms of "bad" or distasteful. We grew up hearing these words from the neighbors and relatives to label something with one or more of the 3 levels, especially Grandpa Gilbertson! The words were uff-da, ish-da and fee-da.

So here goes, using my brother Ronnie's puking incident!
Uff-da = Allen stuck his toe in Ronnie's mouth!
Ish-da = Ronnie puked all over the porch!
Fee-da = The cats are eating it!

In the summer months we went fishing a lot at Lac qui Parle Lake by Milan and usually caught a number of bullheads to bring home to eat. One of us got the bright idea to slip a few into our cattle tank and of course they survived and thrived in there on the various forms of algae and moss in the big water tank. It was alongside the south side of the barn and had about two feet of water, and the bullheads provided us hours of fishing for them with worms from the garden. It was a real nice boredom killer while it lasted.

But all good things come to an end too as the cats also used it to kill boredom once they discovered the fish in there! On more than one occasion, Dad would come home from the field or someplace to find the cattle bellowing in the barnyard because they were thirsty so Dad went right to the water tank and sure enough there would be a dead cat floating on its side stiff as a board, probably having been in there many hours.

There was a board over the tank and the cats would sit or lay on the board and watch the bullheads swimming around and eventually trying to catch one. Sometimes they would somehow lose their grip on the board and in they would go. There was no way they could grab onto the smooth steel tank so once they hit the water it was game over! Since that happened several times to the cattle that was the end of fish in the water tank.

Dad's favorite cat of them all was a big tomcat he named, Thomas. We were never sure that it was even one of ours as we couldn't remember it when it was younger, but one winter it showed up in the barn and in fact the winter time was the only time we saw it.

Thomas would lay on top of the small "milk house" at the end by the first cow and when Dad walked by during chores or milking, Thomas would playfully swat Dad in the face with a paw! His claws were always retracted and he only did this with Dad, maybe because he was taller and within reach. Dad loved telling this story about Thomas the cat and whenever we were all together and someone brought up life on the farm, Dad would talk about "Thomas" the cat!

The cats were always a great source of entertainment for us. And one summer my brother Lynn, got the idea to "parachute" cats off the granary roof using plastic sheets made into crude parachutes. We worked on getting the right size parachute that we thought would work with a cat and picked the cats we would try it on but with absolutely no consideration about what the cats thought about this! There was an attempt to get a cat up on the roof but it was only an "attempt". The cat had the final decision about that! It sure would have been fun though, to see a cat in a parachute!

One of the major hazards to the cats, other than Dad right after they were born, was in the winter time. It didn't take a cold cat long to figure out that the engine compartment of a car was a very cozy place while the engine was warm after being driven!

More than a few times, if we forgot to check the car by pounding on the hood before starting, a cat would get caught in the fan belt or the fan right after starting and we would hear loud thrashing and cat screeching, then silence! Sometimes the cat had only superficial wounds and survived, minus a tail or so but most of the time they were killed. One night when we were visiting at Lowell & Mildred Armstrong's it happened to one of their cats.

It was the sound of the engine starting, then CLANG, CLANG, CLANG, MEEEOOOOW!, some screeching and we saw the cat run out about 20 or 30 feet in the snow and fall over! We ran over to it but it was already dead. It had been cut open by the fan blade and was stringing out guts from the car to where it collapsed! Pretty gross to see.

Usually everyone who had cats had to adjust to pounding on the hood as soon as the weather started getting cold. Engine compartments nowadays are too full of extra stuff to have any room for a cat to take advantage of!

Our Dogs

"Shep" was the first dog we had when we lived by Haydenville. It was a mixed breed with white, black and orange fur. When we moved into Montevideo Shep was taken to my Uncle Lyle's farm ad a couple years later we took him back when we moved back to the farm. He was getting old and sick then and had some near death experiences. One time, when we thought he would die, we dug a large grave for him on the edge of the grove west of the garden. But he pulled through and the "grave" was filled back in. Eventually he got so sick that he would growl and snarl at us if we got too close so Dad finally called a neighbor over to put him down.

Not long after that we got a female mixed breed Collie dog we named Queenie. She was a medium sized wiry dog and would run a lot and chase after us all the time. Her first litter was 14 pups and us kids were sure excited about the prospects of 14 puppies to play with! But we only ended up with one as the rest were given away when they were old enough. I don't think Dad "put" any of them down either, at least I can't remember that he did. While we had all those puppies though, it sure was fun to be "attacked" by them and be swarmed over!

The puppy we kept was appropriately called "Retardo" because one day when it was half-grown he was run over by Grandpa Gilbertson during one of his visits. The dog was okay physically but may have had some brain damage as it was "different" after that. It seemed to stay a puppy permanently and was always sort of goofy acting and perpetually happy all the time, which of course was a good thing I guess.

Queenie was probably the only female dog in the area and when she came in heat then the neighborhood male dogs would come around. Two of which were persistent to the extreme! Severin Hanson's dog was usually the first and on a number of occasions would be seen sneaking across the field to our grove. And if I was armed he provided a good target!

The BB gun never had an effect on him but the .22 rifle did, more from the sound, because I'd never hit him with a bullet. I would empty Dad's rifle at him as he ran back home, the bullets kicking up dust behind him and he would stay home for a while but then would be back again! I considered myself a good shot with the rifle so I probably kept missing him on purpose as the Hansons were our good friends and closest neighbor.

The worst male dog visitor was Elmer Paulson's dog. They lived east of us about 1/2 mile and we never saw the dog coming over because he only "visited" at night. Dad kept Queenie locked in the barn at night while in heat but that didn't stop Paulson's dog! One night we heard strange sounds coming from the barn that sounded like wood ripping apart and whining sounds and by the time Dad got to the barn the dog had chewed a hole right through the barn door to get at Queenie! That was one desperately horny dog!

Dad blocked off the hole so the dog couldn't escape, grabbed a board or something and darn near beat that dog to death! That only worked for a short time as not long after the beating it was back again! I later saw it by the pig house one evening and asked Dad if I could shoot at it with the 20 gauge shotgun. He said okay but just to scare it. I shot right at it from by the house and it had to have been hit by several shotgun pellets as it took off yelping across the field. It never came back!

We attempted to turn Queenie into a hunting dog and would bring her along while hunting pheasants out in our fields. Although she would chase up an initial pheasant or two, at the first shot she would tear off back to the barn to hide!

Almost every night, neighboring dogs, and ours, would "talk" to one another. Dogs from miles around would take turns barking out whatever dogs bark about, and sometimes it went on all night long. I remember being kept awake by Queenie's barking and finally having to "train" her to stop it on command!

When it got real bad, I would get up out of bed, go outside and catch her and give her a few good whacks till she started whining and she would run off and hide, and not bark, at least for a while. This action took place a number of times before she "learned" and then all I had to do was holler "no" and she wouldn't bark the rest of the night.

The same "training" was needed when I started to drive the car and go out on dates. All dogs barked when a car was coming up the driveway and of course this was a good thing for various reasons, one being that we wouldn't be caught off guard peeing in the middle of the yard by a visitor, or being caught by parents doing something naughty while they were gone!

After I started dating and going out on Friday and Saturday nights I, of course, had a curfew which was 10:30 at first. Montevideo had a curfew then of 10:00 PM for 16 and under and midnight for 16-18 years old. At first I obeyed the curfew that Mom and Dad set but only for a while. Since the dog barked when a car came up the driveway, she always let Mom & Dad know when I really got home! When I was late I would get a butt chewing and threats of not getting to go to Montevideo again for a while (grounded)!

I remember getting home late one night and coming down the driveway. Queenie met me just past the grove of trees and barked like mad all the way to the house! I couldn't lie my way out of it when asked next morning about when I got home because they knew! I blamed the dog for my transgressions and some more "training" was required!

Later when I came home late after a night out, I stopped the car as soon as I saw or heard the dog and called her to me. I would then grab her and "educate" her until she took off whining and hiding. This went on for a while until she finally figured this plan out and stopped barking no matter what time it was. She would still bark at other cars coming, just not ours! The folks would still know sometimes when I was real late but not because of Queenie. After her "training" was complete, she would meet me out past the grove and run alongside the car all the way to the house, quiet as a "church mouse".

4-H Club

After moving back out to the farm, we soon joined the local 4-H club which was called the *Mandt Live Wires*. As members, we had to pick projects to be involved in, including a number of various areas involving the home, farming, health. We had to give project reports and physical demonstrations several times a year at our monthly meetings. These meetings were usually held at either the District 31 or District 33 schoolhouses.

Not all the farm families were involved in 4-H but most were and the meetings were as much a social get together as a meeting. I used to dread the meetings where I had to give a project report or demonstrations in front of all the kids and parents. Being very shy in front of anyone, I would become almost physically sick and could hardly talk, but managed to get through them uninjured!

My first major project was raising a pig. I probably had a name for it too but can't remember it after all these years. Dad actually had more to do with raising it than I did but it was mine in name! Maybe I just called it "pig"! Lynn called his pig "Happy".

There wasn't a whole lot to do with raising a pig other than feeding it and keeping it washed and clean and then entering for judging at the Chippewa County fair. Since our hog herd had their litters later than most other farms, my 4-H pig was of course smaller than most all the other pigs being judged. It was particularly embarrassing when all the pigs in the spring litter weight class had to be judged together in one big pen.

We had a cane and a guide board, which was about a 2 foot by 3 foot piece of painted plywood with a handle on it that was used to guide the pig around for the judges and to keep it separated from other pigs. Since my pig was smaller than the other pigs, and sort of like a teenager among adults it had a lot more "energy" than the bigger pigs and as soon as we got it in the judging pen it took off running with me chasing it and trying to get it under control while all the spectators were laughing.

Of course it never stood still for the judges and they probably never saw it anyway. I at least got a white ribbon which was the lowest one given out! I suppose it was pretty funny to see but it sure was embarrassing. After that one year having a pig project I then started a dairy calf project.

My first dairy calf was called "Daisy" and because of her having scar tissue on her udder, points were taken away during judging. I picked another one the following year that I named, "Cindy."

My 4-H heifer, "Cindy." We earned a blue ribbon.

A dairy calf was more work than a pig but at least the calves were more manageable. Besides the feeding and working, they needed more cleaning and grooming, which meant washing and scrubbing her coat and trimming and polishing hooves for show. Since cattle lay down wherever, they usually get shit stuck in their hair and this and the pee stains had to be removed as well as possible.

Once we got the solid matter (shit) scrubbed out we would mix bleach with water and soap and try to bleach out the stains. It only worked so-so and of course the best thing would be to have a calf that was all black but since we had black and white Holstein cattle they always seemed to be more white than black, at least on the "laying down" part of their body!

Another task that took lots of time was training the calf to be "led" with a halter. This was a requirement in the judging area so we could "present" our calf to the judges from different angles. Since cattle were naturally put off by this annoyance and attempt to limit their freedom, we usually had to rely on mechanical means to get the training started! Dad would fire up the tractor and tie the calf behind it 10 or 20 feet back and would drive around the yard while I practiced leading it. The calf would fight it but the tractor was unsympathetic! It probably did work some because I could lead it around for the most part during the county fair judging. It was probably more the calf getting used to me than anything else though.

We had a good amount of success with our dairy calves too. We never got less than a blue ribbon and Lynn's calf won a high enough ribbon to be selected for the state fair one year!

Being farm kids, we lived for the Chippewa County Fair each year in August. The first day was "entry day" for all the 4-H animals and exhibits and one of our neighbors with a truck or trailer would haul the animals to the fair grounds. As soon as we got the animals settled in to their assigned pen or stall spot, off we went to check out the rest of the fair. I was never gone too long though because the animals needed occasional food and water and manure cleaned out and fresh bedding (straw put down).

It was fun sometimes to laugh at and, or, tease the "city" kids as they tried to avoid "cow pies" accidentally left on purpose for them to step in or avoid a cow's pee spray. When we were tired or bored or just showing off for the city kids we sat down and leaned on our calf while they were laying down showing how cool and unafraid we were.

Judging day was always mass confusion as we all were in a rush to get our animals washed and groomed at the last minute. The worst thing that could happen was for the calf to lay down on a pile of shit or a puddle of pee right before going in to be judged.

Our other main hangout at the fair was the midway and my cousin Gary and I spent countless hours in front of the gaming booths and rides. Sometimes we had money and sometimes not but it was always fun. Every evening there was a grandstand show and it didn't take long for our crafty little minds to figure out a way to sneak under the bleachers to look for dropped change. We got chased out occasionally but always seemed to find a dime here and maybe a quarter or two here and there. This supplemented what little we could beg off of our parents.

The small horticultural building where the fruits and vegetables were displayed was an occasional hangout when we were hungry. If the people putting the exhibits on the shelves had no prior experience with us they would always put the nicest looking apples, plums and berries within the easiest reach. If they weren't watching them or were distracted, well you get the picture. They sure were good fruits. All blue ribbon winners in our minds.

There was one incident that happened on the midway that I will never forget. I was with my family one night and since we were together we must have been getting ready to go home. My sister Nancy was fourteen years old and very particular about how she looked to the boys! She had just got a new fall coat and we were all standing near the tilt-a-whirl ride and it was going full speed and riders were screaming and all of a sudden this long sheet of pronto pup and cotton candy infused vomit came flying out from one of the cars and it made a direct hit on Nancy!

She had puke all over her new coat and in her hair and on about everything else she was wearing. She started screaming and crying and Mom and Dad were trying to clean it off of her and people standing around and watching or laughing. She was SO embarrassed! Better her than me though!! To this day I can point right to the spot where that happened.

On the last evening of the fair and before the evening grandstand show we would take part in the parade of 4-H cattle in front of the grandstand. One year, as we were waiting in line with our calves when Lynn's calf, got scared of something and bolted away and took off galloping down the race track we were on, running past all the cattle towards the front of the procession and past the grandstand and out into the infield. There were a bunch of men and older boys chasing after it and finally someone managed to grab a hold of the halter lead rope and got it under control. Again, we managed to provide the public with some great humor and entertainment. It seems that we never had any problems standing out in a crowd!!!

Our 4-H Club formed a square-dance group one year and we traveled around the local area and performed at various events including the grandstand at the county fair. It consisted of the older kids in the club and since there were more big girls than boys, the bigger girls had to dress like a guy and wear a white shirt, bow tie and pants where the girl dancers wore the fluffy square dance skirt and blouse.

And they also had to pack their hair under the cowboy hat to look even more manly! Our music was provided by Axel Larson (another relative) with his violin. He also played for adult square dance groups too and was very good. I guess we were quite a hit with it too but we did it for only one year. Nancy had to be a guy dancer. Ha!

I guess the most important part of being in the 4-H club, to me, was our softball team. I just couldn't wait till spring came and we could start practicing for the upcoming season. We practiced and played our "home" games at the ball field at the District 33 School which was about 2 1/2 miles south of our farm. We played teams from Rosewood Township, who were our biggest rival, and Montevideo, Milan, Big Bend and one or two others. I guess my pitching reputations preceded me and I was also the main pitcher on this team also. It was very rare that we lost a game, due mainly to the competitive make-up of the players.

During the five years I played, my teammates consisted of Albie Gilsrud, Denny Skogrand, Joey Lynne, Galen Rud, Rick Skogrand, Wayne Skogrand, and several others I can't recall. Each team also had to have one girl playing during the game and since girls didn't play anything competitively back then, they weren't very good at all so we had them playing in right field where almost no balls were hit! Marie Kvistero, and Jane Rud were among the only girls that dared to play on the team and who could tolerate our male disdain at their poor batting and fielding!

I have to "toot my own horn" a bit in stating that I was the pitcher because I was better at it than the other players!! Denny was a better shortstop. Galen was a better catcher and Joey was a better 2nd baseman but I was a better pitcher so we all had our certain place on the team. I had the standard fast pitch wind-up and could vary my pitches between a fastball, slider, or a curveball and always had a high number of strikeouts in every game. Because striking out every batter I faced was my goal, I had no mercy on any of them, to include younger, inexperienced, poor players and girls. I felt absolutely no guilt at all in blowing three straight curveball strikes by a poor batter who didn't swing until the pitch was already in the catcher's mitt!

Because of my competitive nature, I had sort of a running feud with some of the parents, especially those of opposing teams and had to listen to constant yelling of "pitch it so they can hit it" or words to that effect and if they got loud enough, our coach (a parent) would stop the game and pull me off to the side and convince me to pitch slow enough that they could hit. So I would try to let them hit and since I sucked terribly at trying to pitch slow, I sometimes ended up giving up a walk and then got pissed off over it, so I took it out on the next batter!

To pitch like I did took lots of practice and I spent a lot of time, almost every day doing it. At home I outlined a strike zone on the side of our granary above a home plate and would practice my pitches against imaginary batters. Since I had only one softball, it was lots of walking back and forth. Sometimes I would convince Lynn or Ronnie to be the batter but they were always scared of getting hit by one of my pitches!

The Garden

Just west of the house, past the lawn, was our garden. It was approximately 50' by 50' so wasn't very big but we still managed to grow enough vegetables to last us through to the next summer. Mom always canned some tomatoes and beans and sweet corn and peas. She also canned a lot of fruits like peaches, apricots, and pears for sauce and these, of course, were our favorites to eat. We didn't grow them so they were purchased by the crate at the grocery store in Montevideo.

Another one of the chores I was given was to weed the garden. As much as I hated it, though, there was a payoff in being able to "graze" while I pulled weeds! Beans & peas never taste better than when they are fresh picked and eaten in the garden and I would fill myself up first before I filled the bucket! This was especially so when I was told to go to the strawberry patch north of the grove to pick some for dessert. Of course Mom would bitch at me for not bringing enough back to the house but more times than not, I had eaten most of what I picked and there weren't any more ripe ones left!

We also had a large potato patch in the field just south of the pig house. In the spring Dad would plow it up and would get a gunny sack full of seed potatoes that we had to cut up in sections so that there was at least one "eye" or potato shoot in each section. These we then would insert into the bottom side of the furrow Dad had just plowed up with the three bottom plow. After this was done, Dad would then plow this over, creating a new furrow about four feet away and we would then plant this row. We probably did four or five rows this way and it produced enough potatoes to last us a year.

The absolute worst part of growing potatoes, though, was harvesting them and since they grew underground they had to be dug up by hand with a potato fork or a 5-tine pitchfork. And since they had no set pattern of growth, they had to be searched for which meant lots of extra digging. On occasion Dad would run the plow through a row or two of potatoes and would turn them up to the surface but lots of them got reburied so we had to dig for them anyway. After harvesting them we put them in gunny sacks and stored them down in the cellar where they kept pretty good through the winter and following summer.

Cucumbers: Our Cash Crop!

One year, when I was a teenager, the Gedney pickle company started up a collection center in Appleton, a small town about 15 miles west for cucumbers for their pickling plants. They furnished the seeds for any farmers who agreed to plant them and harvest and bring the cucumbers in. Dad, of course, jumped right on this deal and so we had a cucumber patch just east of our grove, of about an acre in size. Even though it was good money, another reason I think Dad had was to attempt to keep my brothers and I occupied with something other than screwing off and getting into trouble!

I was used to doing lots of chores and field work but this was absolutely the worst because I had to pick cukes in my spare time! Since cucumbers are a vine plant they spread out on the ground under a low canopy of large leaves that shield the cucumber from the hot sun. The only way to pick them is by crawling on knees through them and searching for them, and doing this day after day is no fun for kids to do.

The cucumbers are graded by size, the smallest being the most valuable so the more bushel baskets of smaller ones meant more money for us, but they were also harder to locate and pick as they blended in with foliage better than bigger ones.

A typical day went like this:

Dad: "You boys hurry up now and get those cucumbers picked."
Us: "Yeah O.K., we will."
Dad: "Come on now, I told you boys a half hour ago to get started before it gets too hot!"
Us: "We're going, jeez!"
Dad: "Huh!!! If you want some spending money you get out there right now."

Us: "We already picked some! It's too hot." (Grumble, moan!)

Dad: "Huh! Well, I guess I'm going to have to pick em then or it'll never get done." (Guilt trip.) Huh!

So then we would really feel guilty for a while and fill up a few baskets. It went on like this most every day! The payoff though was pretty good as us kids got to spend most of what we made.

When we filled enough bushel baskets, off we went to Appleton where we waited in line till we got up to the conveyor belt. Then we would dump all the baskets and the cucumbers were automatically sorted by size into different baskets. They were then weighed and tallied up and we got paid on the spot. We made about two trips a week there.

I finally started to take the cukes myself since I had just got my driver's license and Dad trusted me enough. I would take the back seat out of the 1956 Plymouth and stack bushel baskets there and in the trunk, and in the front seat too to take up all the room in the car so my brothers couldn't go along. Ha! I was able to take around 13-15 bushel baskets that way.

One of the worst things about cucumbers is all the little spiny stickers all over their skin. Our hands were always raw from them and from the little spines on the underside of the leaves and on the stems. Cucumber juice mixed with dirt was extremely hard to wash off our hands and Dad had some sort of biodegradable solution that we had to use full strength for it to work at all. I was thinking one day that since this stuff works just O.K., then Hi-Lex bleach should work even better, since everyone knew that "Hi-Lex bleach gets your whites like new, so it has to be the one for you!" or words to that effect!

I had some sort of plans for that Friday night and figured that I needed really clean hands for whatever it was I was going to do. So I got the gallon jug of bleach and proceeded to pour it on my hands. It took about two seconds before I realized my mistake, but too late now! My hands started stinging and I immediately stuck them in water, and they did appear to be a little cleaner than before but the odor of bleach was the worst part. It took about a week for the smell to get out of my skin. Mom & Dad were pissed about it and it also affected any plans I had for that weekend because the bleach smell was so intense that I didn't dare go out of embarrassment.

Some of our neighbors raised cucumbers also. Pete and Severin Hanson, who lived just west of us, grew them one year but they were both in their 70s and couldn't get on their hands & knees so they just walked through the patch and would bend down to pick the ones they could see. They only saw the big ones which they picked but since those were the least valuable, they hardly made any money at it.

Chapter 5

Shopping in Montevideo

We were pretty self-sustaining on the farm with the hog butchering, chickens, eggs, milk, garden produce and such, but for anything else we mostly shopped in Montevideo. This was a Friday night ritual for us along with most other farm families, as the stores stayed open until 9:00 PM.

Since we couldn't afford to eat out back then, we ate an early supper and then loaded up the egg crates and took off for town. Our first stop was the creamery on the north end of Main Street where we would sell the eggs and pick up a check for the milk we sold the previous week.

The next stop was Johnnie's grocery store a block west of Main Street by the Farmer's Union Co-op. They had pretty much all other food items we needed, and after that it was off to the wonders of all the different stores on Main Street.

Dad would drive up and down Main Street until a parking spot was empty (parking was easier in the parking lots in the back alley but the primary reason to park on Main Street was to people watch!). And us kids were usually out the door before he came to a stop!

I would head immediately to the closest dime store to our parking spot to check out the toy aisle for the latest toy or the candy aisle to see how much I could get with my allowance. It didn't take very long to spend it either and it was usually on candy.

The toy selection back in the 50s was nowhere what it is now as the toy aisle was just that. One aisle with toys usually on only one side. Everything was mechanical too, no electronics.

Ben Franklin and *Woolworth's* were the two five and dime stores in Montevideo, but we called them the "dime" stores. They were variety stores with a little bit of everything.

After visiting those two stores, it was on to any other store that had candy, toys, or guns, and also comic books we couldn't live without. *Rexall* and *Zenk Drugs* had a pretty good comic and paperback book selections so I would always spend some time there reading new comic books until I got told by a clerk to either buy or leave!

Coast to Coast had some rifles and shotguns to gawk over and a good selection of BB guns they would let us handle, and where we bought enough BBs to get through the next week.

All in all, Main Street was a pretty neat place to be on Friday nights. The stores were filled with shoppers, and friends and neighbors engaging in small talk and kids running on the sidewalks and in the stores. And of all the many stores, there were no office business on Main Street like there is nowadays. All the stores were retail stores only.

Most of the time I was with my cousin Gary Armstrong and if we weren't getting into trouble ourselves we would meet other kids around our age from either other country schools or 4-H or whatever and probably cause some more trouble! This would usually involve peashooters, because they were cheap to buy, and there were lots of targets on Main Street too. We picked on the town kids more than anyone else too. One Friday evening in the summer we got the bright idea to climb up on one of the store roofs down by the Hollywood Theater. It was probably 35-40 feet tall.

On the way down there we caught a fair number of frogs which we stuffed in our pants pockets. So we're up on the roof edge over Main Street and cars were, as usual, bumper to bumper "dragging main" in both directions. Along came a convertible full of teenage boys & girls and what a tempting frog target that was! So we started pitching live frogs down at the car and after missing at first, managed to land a few in the front & back seats. Ha! The guys started swearing and the girls started screaming and of course they looked up and saw us so we hightailed it out of there because we figured they would come looking for us. That sure was fun! That incident was rather typical of the stunts we pulled.

Montevideo had its share of "odd" people too. Probably the most odd and started-at person was the "cigarette lady". We called her that because she would continuously walk up & down both sidewalks of Main Street and look for cigarette butts that were long enough to re-light and smoke. She was always well-dressed, but in the style of the 1940s. Always in long fashionable black slacks and high heels and a hat, and had a certain swagger in her stride. The most noticeable feature about her though, and why she was stared at by passers-by, was that she was burnt real bad in a fire a number of years before and the skin on her face and hands had been damaged. Sort of darker tan and splotchy and wrinkled real bad. She never talked to anyone that we saw, but Dad, who had known her before her accident always said "hello" to her in passing and she always responded back in kind.

Then there was this kid who had real thick "coke bottle" glasses and had to hold a comic book right against his glasses to read! He was always worth a minute or two of a rude stare! And an older guy with no nose and several others that were unusually noticeable! They were all a part of the Friday nights in Monte.

"Al's" popcorn stand was a main fixture on Main Street too. He was a middle-aged man and his little stand was almost right next to the Hollywood Theater. We always had to stop there and either buy some candy or get a small bag of his popcorn which was the best we had ever tasted.

Mom & Dad usually finished up any shopping by around 8:00 PM. Then the next hour or so was usually spent sitting in the car and watching people walk by. It was the weekly social event as friends, acquaintances, or relatives walking, would stop and visit for a while to hear the latest news or gossip from the last week.

I very clearly remember a Friday night in November 1963, the day President Kennedy was assassinated. We needed groceries and had to take the eggs in so we went to town. The mood of the few people out was so somber. Adults and even kids were walking around either crying or teary-eyed and people didn't talk to anyone except to maybe say hello! What an extremely sad time.

Every so often we got to take in a movie after shopping was over. Mom & Dad enjoyed going to see them and if a good one was playing, then we went. There was only one movie a week at the Hollywood Theater and it usually started about 7:30. Back then with the price of one ticket a person could actually sit through both showings of the movie and many times we would go in and get seated during maybe the last 10-15 minutes or half hour left of the first showing.

We then sat through the intermissions, cartoons, and the next showing until the part of the movie that was showing when we sat down came up. If it was a while before the end we then left and headed for home. If close to the end then we sometimes stayed to see the end again. That was common in those days. Now the theaters are cleaned out after each showing.

The *Hollywood Theater* had a concession stand but it only had candy and no soda fountain. There was a pop dispensing machine in the right hallway which, for a dime would dispense a 6 or 8 ounce cup and fill it with whatever pop flavor was chosen. My favorite was a flavor called Green River. It was, of course, green in color and came either carbonated or non-carbonated and no ice either.

Since the cups were small it had to be sipped on slowly to last. That was the only place I ever saw that *Green River* pop sold and to this day can still remember the taste! I can't remember if the concession stand sold popcorn, but I do remember buying it at Al's popcorn stand and taking it in the theater.

On the nights that we didn't go to a show, the last stop before heading home was the little "Dairy Freeze" shop on the north end of Main Street. They had maybe five or six or so flavors of hard ice cream and we would each get a cone for the 20 minute ride home. Another Friday night ritual that we did, summer or winter!

Sometimes, in the summer, we would go to a movie out at the, *Starlite Drive-in Theater* by the golf course. This, again, meant a stop at *Al's Popcorn Stand* for bags of his wonderful popcorn. We would get parked and hang the speaker from a window and, if it was a while before the movie started, us kids would take off and go to the concession stand or run around with other kid friends.

Rural Stores

About 4 miles east of our farm at the intersection of Hwy 40 and Hwy 29 going to Benson, were two stores across the highway from each other. *Burgess Store,* which was actually two parts, one being the grocery store and the other room being the beer joint were connected together by a doorway. We didn't go to the *Burgess Store* much because I don't think Mom wanted us kids to see people drinking beer in the bar. Ha! There was also horseshoe pits out back and in the summertime they had weekly horseshoe tournaments and leagues.

We did most of our shopping at the *Coss Store* as they had a better selection of groceries and also a small selection of hardware and farm machinery items. Before the Tom Coss family bought it, it was owned and operated by a man in a wheelchair.

Chapter 6

My Cousin Gary

Gary Armstrong and me at Gary's farm in 1957

My best friend and companion in my pre-teen years on the farm was my first cousin Gary Armstrong. He is the only son of Dad's sister Mildred and her husband Lowell Armstrong. His older sisters are Janet, Joanne and Sharon. He is one year younger than me.

Their farm place was west of us across the section and 1 1/2 miles by road since we both had 1/4 mile driveways. Their driveway was just a dirt road through the field and since my uncle never graveled it, it was near impossible to drive on it in the spring. There were a few times when we visited them that we had to park and walk up to the house and Mom didn't appreciate that at all! So there were times that the condition of their driveway kept us home or them home!

As a young child I can't recall playing with Gary until we moved back out to the farm after living in Montevideo. In fact I can't recall Gary in grade school even though we went to the same country one-room school, but our companionship and escapades and adventures all took place away from school.

We usually took turns going over to each other's place to play or do stuff on an occasional Saturday. When Gary came to our place we would play "Cowboys & Indians" or "Cops & Robbers" with Lynn & Ronnie, and then go off hunting with our BB guns, or play with cats or dogs or shoot at pigs or chickens, or go up to Hanson's grove and explore or whatever came to mind! When I went to Gary's it was only the two of us and the options were different there.

When I couldn't get Dad to drive me over to their farm I would either walk through the fields straight across the section or ride my bike on the gravel roads. Riding bike was easy and fast if the road was smooth and hard, but real tough to do when the gravel was loose.

We always had our trusty BB guns and plenty of BBs and one of the first things we did was to hike over to two vacant groves of trees in the middle of their section to see what we could shoot at there. These groves are halfway between their farm and the Mandt Church, which no longer stands as it was torn down in 2003.

One time we were there, we spotted a big grey squirrel in a tree and started shooting at it. Our BB guns weren't very powerful and the BBs would just hit it but would bounce off. Since we both had plenty BBs we kept at it for an hour or two, when finally I think the squirrel succumbed to the shock of being hit so many times by BBs that it finally fell to the ground stunned. We immediately clubbed it to death and decided that we were hungry and would skin and eat it! We first castrated it though, because we were boys, and marveled at the fact that this small squirrel had bigger balls than we did!!

One of us had matches so we finally got a fire going and got it ready for cooking. We stuck a green tree branch through it and then took turns roasting it over the fire. We were really anticipating a great feast for us mighty hunters but after a taste or two we gave up on it because it really tasted like crap! It might have been better if we had salt & pepper but it was mainly the flavor of squirrel which we had never tasted before. Yuk!

One of our favorite things to do at Gary's was to go "swimming" in the hog wallows in the pasture behind their grove. After rains these wallows would sometimes be two or three feet deep and perfect for us to swim in, naked, of course! And the water was warm.

Once, when we were in swimming, my sister Nancy and Gary's sister Sharon snuck up on us and stole our clothes and took off running back to the house with Gary and I hot on their heels, naked of course, and screaming our heads off at them. We never caught them but sure caught hell from Gary's mom Mildred when she saw us with no clothes on and the girls nowhere to be seen! They finally gave them back to us though after they tired of laughing at us and teasing us!

Another time when we were in swimming the herd of pigs came over to wait their turn when they spotted our clothes on the ground and immediately started to drag them around and fight over them! Here were pigs playing tug-o-war with our clothes. Squealing and running around in circles, and Gary and I chasing them, naked of course, trying to pull our clothes away and finally losing the battle!

All our clothes were eventually completely shredded to pieces including my favorite "fish" shirt, as seen in the picture of me, my brothers and sister all sitting on the fence at our farm. I didn't care about the rest of the clothes but was sure heartbroken over losing that shirt.

Of course the pigs got paid back shortly thereafter because after we got re-clothed with Gary's wardrobe, we armed ourselves with our trusty BB guns and went pig hunting. Ha! We got our revenge.

When Gary and I were a little older and started shooting our dads' .22 caliber rifles, one of our favorite pastimes was to shoot at Tosten Laumb's silo top about a half mile away! We finally got to where we could hit it most of the time by aiming high in the air over it and lofting a bullet towards it. We could tell when we hit it by hearing a distant "clang" of the bullet impacting the galvanized steel round rooftop of the silo. It was an abandoned farm place so we didn't worry about ricochets! It was fun!

I first learned how to smoke cigarettes with Gary! We were in Montevideo shopping on a Friday night and I was with Gary when we ran into Gary Evenson, an earlier friend of mine when we lived in town. Gary Evenson and I went to Ramsey school together in 2nd grade and they lived not far from our house. All three of us went down to the old train yard where Gary Evenson produced a pack of cigarettes. We all lit one up and then dared each other to "inhale". That was the start of smoking for me. I didn't really like it but it was the "cool" thing to do so we did it as much as we could. Since Lowell and my dad both smoked, half-smoked butts were usually available but we much preferred whole cigarettes and the only way to get them was to "liberate" them.

We first started doing that by sneaking into cars parked down in the parking lots behind Main Street. No one ever locked cars back then and we would take turns sneaking into a car, while the other kept a look out, and rummage through the glove box where we would sometimes find a partial or full pack.

I used to hide my cigarettes up in our granary under the eaves in a small compartment I discovered. But after a few packs were eaten by mice I kept them in a plastic box, and that hiding spot is also still there.

Gary was pretty spoiled as a kid and teenager so he got his way with just about anything with his parents. He smoked up in his room and they knew it but just ignored it. We were over visiting them one night and Gary lit up while we were upstairs and I eventually dared to also and of course my parents found out about it and did I ever catch hell when we got home. I was grounded for quite a while after that. But it didn't stop me from smoking.

As a young kid and a teenager I was fanatical about basketball and played any chance I could. Before I knew what basketball was I could only imagine how it was played by what I heard on the local radio station when they broadcast the Montevideo Mohawk basketball games. Without ever seeing a game played, I thought that it took place in a large walled-off room because I had never seen a gymnasium or a basketball court. Gary had been to games with his older sisters and tried to explain it to me but it never made sense till I finally got to go to a game myself, and that was the most awesome thing I had ever seen!

Finally the day came when I got my own basketball hoop and net and I fastened it to a homemade backboard and nailed it about nine or ten feet off the ground on a tree by the house and there I would spend hours, even in the winter, shooting baskets and imagining I was one of the local high school stars winning the game at the buzzer! When in the winter I would shovel off the snow and play with a ball that wouldn't bounce because of the cold. When my hands got so could I couldn't feel the ball then I quit.

Basketball heaven happened for Gary and me when his dad Lowell gave us permission to clean out the hay mow in the upstairs of their big barn and to make a fairly accurate basketball court out of it. It had a nearly smooth wood floor on which we had painted a free-throw line, and with a real hoop and net we were in business. We played for hours and hours even in the winter again during the official basketball season.

We had to wear gloves and coats in the barn and our breath was a continuous white steam because it was that cold, but we didn't care. We were real stars, in our minds, and would pretend we were various high school stars that we watched on TV during the state basketball tournament at Williams Arena. Those games were almost magical for us and we watched every one we could after school let out on Friday. This was where we learned and honed our considerable basketball skills, within our own minds! The "games" we each took turns "winning" with a last second shot were countless!

Randy Stay, who became my best friend in my teenage years lived a couple miles northwest of us and he also had made a basketball court up in their big barn. So we also spent time there a lot playing ball. Sometimes we would meet up and travel over to a farm in West Bank Township where there were some other farm kids who had made a real fancy court in their barn. Our team played their team and we would get our butts beat good by them. And we thought we were so good!

One day I decided to reposition the basketball hoop on the side of the granary to keep me from having to chase the ball all the time. Since we didn't have a ladder (or maybe we did) I got the bright idea of using the tractor to do it because it was the right height. Dad was gone that day and because of wintertime he had drained the radiator. I thought that all I had to do was fill the radiator with hot water, it would start and I would be in business. Well, I cranked and cranked with the hand crank and it wouldn't fire for me. About that time Dad came home and laid into me for almost ruining the engine! It would have sure been a mess if the water had frozen and expanded inside the engine. Live and learn!

Being typical farm boys Gary and I always had our BB guns within easy reach and hardly went anywhere without them. And when we couldn't think of or find anything else to shoot at, we decided that we would have BB gun fights! We would get our parents' heavy winter coats out, bundle up in them and shoot at each other. How freaking stupid we were! Luckily we never got hurt from it although the BBs did sting even through thick coats. And we each still have two eyes!

Not far removed from BB gun fights were the notorious shit fights. This usually involved me, Gary and Lynn & Ronnie, four lengths of fencing laths and numerous piles of fresh cow shit all over the barnyard. We would at least be smart enough to take our shirts off before and we would run around chasing each other with the stick full of fresh cow shit and be splattering each other until we were covered in it! We didn't ever use pig shit though as that was real nasty stuff and was declared off-limits.

It really was great fun though and when we tired of it the cattle tank was the first choice to wash off the shit! Bad move! The cattle then wouldn't drink from it and when Dad came home from fieldwork and saw bellowing cattle around the water tank, one look was all he needed to see why they were thirsty and of course we caught hell over that! After that we used the water pump!

When summer arrived and the 4th of July was getting close, Gary and I would practically do anything and everything to get our hands on fireworks. We begged and begged our parents to make the annual trip to South Dakota to get us some. We usually succeeded because Dad couldn't wait to get some also! Fireworks were illegal in Minnesota then and still are now except for small ground fireworks. We would get several large packs of *Black Cat* firecrackers, which we thought were the best, and some bottle rockets.

Almost anything was a possible victim or target for us! We would fashion water cannons out of tin cans and spend hours launching these at each other from about 20 yards or so, then it was on to blowing up ant hills, or an unlucky frog or something like that! Chickens were always fun with bottle rockets too.

One time when my cousin Duwayne Underthun was over, we caught several sparrows that were roosting in our barn and Duwayne said he would show me something really "neat". It was dark out so he grabbed a sparrow, and wedged a firecracker down its throat so it couldn't spit it out, then lit the fuse and let it fly off. All we could see was a small trail of sparks off in the distance, then bam, a bright light flashed a distance away in the pitch black night! That really was "neat" but cruel.

Back to the doing anything for fireworks. The aunts, uncles, cousins and Grandpa and Grandma had an annual family picnic up at Scandinavian Lake. There was a year where Gary and I had either shot up our fireworks or didn't' get any so we are doing the lake thing, either fishing off the dock or looking for trouble to get into, when this carload of older teenagers come rolling up by the resort store. They all got out and started blowing up firecrackers all over and having lots of fun doing it and showing off in front of us too!

Of course, we were observant enough to see that they kept their firecrackers in the glove compartment. They left but came back later and this time they parked on the side of the store out of sight from the front and they all went in the store. We wasted no time to even think it out and immediately snuck up to the passenger side of the car, reached in, grabbed all the firecrackers they had and took off out in the woods behind the store. They had good fireworks and lots of them and we were in hog heaven!

We hid out for most of the afternoon until it was time to go swimming at Lake Linka. When we dared venture back, their car was gone and what a relief that was as we knew they knew who took their stuff! Not many opportunities slipped by us. I still have a permanent scar on my back from the time Gary threw a lit firecracker at me which blew up just as it hit my back.

One of our main adventure spots during the summer was the big gravel pit about a mile northeast of our farm. There was also an old abandoned farm house once owned by the "Chistifa" family or something approaching that name. We used to rummage through the house as it was full of forgotten items in all the rooms and old crinoline dresses in the closets and old furniture. It was like whoever lived there pulled up stakes and left everything they owned. Anyway we had great times going through all that stuff and bringing some of it home and probably destroying the rest, which nowadays was probably a small fortune in antiques!

Anyway, back to the gravel pit. There was one large deep pit, always full of water where we hung out. We found some old boards and once made a raft out of them and we would either float around on that, or dog paddle around the pond as best we could seemingly oblivious to the fact that if one of us ever went under we were "toast"! There was no way any of us could save anyone in trouble with our limited skills in water!

Dad always threatened us to never go over there to play but of course that was then a challenge to us! When Gary and I were old enough to have .22 rifles we would sometimes bring them up there and either shoot at cans or bottles we had thrown in the pit or at garden snakes we would catch and throw out in the water. The snakes would sort of "blow up" when hit by a bullet! Yes, we were cruel to animals!

Another of Gary Armstrong's and my "moments" was when we were really getting the urge to drive cars and we discovered that Grandpa Gilbertson always left his keys in his car at church! This proved to be too much a temptation so we finally got up the nerve to start it up, it being a 1953 Ford Fairlane with manual transmission. So we did that on and off for several weeks before we finally dared to put it in gear and back it out and back in the parking space behind the church. That then escalated to driving it around in a circle before parking it again and no one being the wiser. We never got caught either by our parents or Grandpa!

A contributing influence to this little prank of ours could have been from boldness due to the after effects of having a wine-buzz from our acolyte duties in church during communion services, which will be the next story.

Again, the reader of these tales (true though) must realize by now that me, my cousin, and my brothers were quite the wild ones and were capable of accomplishing about any sort of mayhem we could think of and damn the consequences. We were wild little "shits". Some would probably say we were out of control! And then lots of these actions could have been due to the fact that our "dorsal lateral prefrontal cortex" - the region of our brain that controls and weighs consequences was not even close to being developed at our young ages! Yes, what a great excuse!

Our main duty and contribution as pre-teens and early teenagers to Mandt Church was as acolytes. I'm not exactly sure of my age when I did it but it must have been around 13-14. I first was an acolyte with Randy Stay, him being a year older, and then with my cousin Gary, him being a year younger so it figures that it was a two year duty. We had our white robes to wear during services where we would light the various candles used, and then once a month we carried the wine trays to and from the altar to the back office to be refilled if necessary during communion services.

Our first taste of the forbidden wine (we couldn't take communion until we were confirmed) started when we brought the used trays to the back for new trays. If the assistant Agnes Rear wasn't looking, we would quickly drain the small wine glasses that some people left half full. And if trays still had full glasses left those were also downed behind her back. Being young as we were it didn't take many partial and some full little communion glasses to get a buzz on! Agnes Rear was also the organist so as soon as communion was over she had to get back to the organ for the next song and thus left us to clean up! Kind of like the fox in the chicken coop, or kids in a candy store! Then we progressed up to taking swigs from the last open wine bottle.

We almost got caught once when doing that and I know she suspected us doing it and would try to keep an extra eye on us. Mom did grab me once after church and demanded to know if I had wine on my breath. I told her, "Yes, I wanted to know what it tasted like because I would be confirmed the next year!" I got chewed on but then it was forgotten.

Several years later, when Gary and I had our driver's licenses, and when either my dad or Gary's dad Lowell let us take a car on a Saturday afternoon we sometimes went on the prowl for junk cars in abandoned farm places. We had heard through the teen grapevine that auto junk yards would pay money for old batteries and radiators and it didn't takes us long to take advantage of that.

Back then, when a farm family's car would wear out it would be towed out in the grove and just left to rust away and almost every farm place had at least one in the woods. We would pick an area of the country and just drive around the mile sections until we came upon an abandoned farm. It was easiest to see the cars in the fall or spring before leaves formed and snow melted. If we spotted a car we would check out the nearest occupied farm to see if they could see us. Then we would park our car out of sight and go and check out the car. Sometimes someone else had beaten us to it but not always.

Batteries were easy to pull and radiators were more labor intensive but we usually had a wrench or socket for any occasion so nothing took very long. We then took what we scavenged in to Montevideo to Flinn's Salvage where we would get a dollar or two per battery (lead) and $5.00 for a radiator, because they were almost all copper. It was great spending money for us.

Chapter 7

Hunting

More appropriately titled "Killing anything that walked, crawled or flew", of which I became very adept at over time! A farm boy never went far without a BB gun in his hand and I got my first one as a Christmas present the first year after we moved back out to the farm. I was eleven years old. To this day, I still think that that was the best present I ever got for Christmas and can still recall the excitement of that moment of unwrapping it but knowing beforehand from pre-Christmas snooping what it was. Along with it were two packs of BBs in the red top crimped tubes which held probably 100 BBs each. The gun itself was a standard lever action which was fairly easy to cock and the BB tube held about a whole pack of BBs. Shaking the gun up and down with the tube full of BBs was music to my ears!

I had a bad experience with a lever action BB gun a year or two earlier on a shopping trip to Montevideo that I'll never forget. There was a general store in town right next to Artigas Plaza that also carried BB guns and while the folks were looking around in the front of the store, I was towards the side where the BB guns were. I was busy gawking at the guns and building up the courage to touch one.

That led to me holding one and aiming it around which then led to attempting to cock it. Unfortunately, there wasn't a store clerk around or I wouldn't have dared to try it! I almost got it to the cocking position when my strength gave out and the lever slammed back down to the stock and somehow also pinned my thumb onto the trigger which had pierced the skin. So there I was screaming for help with this BB gun attached to my bleeding thumb and Mom and Dad and the store clerk in an uproar and other shoppers gawking at the commotion. Dad finally freed my thumb and was mad at me and the store for having the BB guns within reach of kids. I never much cared for lever action guns after that and only had my first one a year or so before I got a pump gun.

It didn't take long to graduate from shooting at cans and bottles to shooting at living things, and this eventually included anything that moved, but I never shot at our cats or dogs. The list included any bird (except robins), frogs, pigs, cows, chickens and even bumble bees! Barn swallows were off limits too as Dad threatened to take my gun away if he ever caught me shooting at them. Birds were my main target through and there was an endless supply of them, mostly sparrows. Our cats were always well fed as that was my justification for shooting so many birds. I used to set up shooting stations at each window in the pig house and spread corn out on the pasture to lure blackbirds within range and then shoot them when they landed to feed!

Grandpa and Grandma Weckhorst had a big barn on their farm by Louisburg and there was a good sized flock of pigeons that hung out there that were big and easy targets for me. I would slowly creep up to the hay mow (2nd floor) and shoot at one before they all flew out. A little while later they would all fly back in to be shot at again. Since they were bigger birds they were harder to kill and many were just wounded. Once in a while one would just be "wing shot" and couldn't fly so my brother and I would catch it and bring it home with us as a pet pigeon!

Mom and Dad were okay with that as it probably would keep us busy enough to stay out of some other trouble! We would fashion a "cage" out of a large cardboard box and with cut out "bars," it worked pretty good. We fed them corn and water and they did fine as we never had one die on us. Every once in a while one would escape and fly off after it had healed up from being shot.

One time when our neighbors Severin, Tillie and Pete Hanson were visiting, we had one pigeon in a cage in the house and we decided to take it out and show it off. Well, it got loose and was flying around in the house banging against walls and windows with us kids trying to catch it, Mom and Dad pissed at us and the Hansons ducking away from the out of control pigeon. We finally caught it but not before it flew over Tillie and "dumped" a load on her shoulder! That was the end of pigeons in the house. Tillie still laughed about that many years later.

Mom's uncle Aslak Skordahl and his wife Lydia lived up in Northwood, N.D. and we went up to visit them once when I was eleven or twelve. They owned a store where they sold clothes and footwear, so the kids got discounts on new shoes and I got a pair of engineer boots. The leather was real thick on them and sometime later when I was back home, I was sitting out on the cistern one day with my BB gun.

I was bored so I decided to shoot the top of my foot, knowing that my tough engineer boots would keep me from any harm! I took the shot and almost blacked out from the pain of the BB hitting my boot and my foot inside. The BB didn't penetrate but the impact and force against my foot caused unbelievable pain. Another lesson learned!

Sometimes, when I was really bored I would take the 20 gauge shotgun out in the woods and shoot it straight overhead and then stand under the lead shot coming down on me through the tree branches. It stung a little but was "sweet pain"!

Before I could use a real gun, I had to "learn" the right and safe way to handle one, and, other than my BB gun, this was done by observing my dad and uncles during our numerous pheasant hunts. That was the way of it and also how they learned while young. At first, since I couldn't carry a gun, I was a "game bearer" and had the "honor" of carrying dead birds that the group had shot down! I quickly learned that was no fun. I also was taught the art of "neck wringing" wounded pheasants that were still very alive but couldn't fly after being shot down.

Eventually, when I became proficient in handling my BB gun safely, I was allowed to carry it on the pheasant hunts and would also shoot it at flushed pheasants, all the while being observed by the adults in the proper handling of it as if it were real. Dad finally taught me to shoot his .22 caliber Remington pump rifle when I was around 12 or 13 years old.

That was a whole other ballgame as far as shooting guns goes and after I became fairly proficient in handling and shooting it, I would sneak it out and go hunting with it, unknown to Dad. Of course .22 bullets and their acquisition by underage kids was always a problem but visits to stores that sold them (though not to us) usually proved fruitful as we had our ways of acquiring them!

About that same time and a little later, I graduated to Dad's 20 gauge single shot shotgun and Dad and I walked out to the northeast field that bordered our pasture. Dad set up a can or something on a fencepost and handed me the shotgun. Then he told me to load it and shoot at the target. I cocked the hammer back and took somewhat of an aim.

I was really nervous and scared but I pulled the trigger and immediately landed on my ass wondering what the hell had happened! The first lesson I learned at that moment was that I fired it off balance with my feet side by side. I learned after that to step into the shot and I know Dad saw my mistake, but what better way to learn! After that, I was finally a responsible hunter and got to go "loaded" on pheasant hunts.

Pheasant hunting season was a glorious time and much looked forward to each fall. Dad's cousin Walter Gilbertson always came down from Minneapolis for the pheasant opener and always brought me, Lynn and Ronnie some bottles of *Sundrop* pop! We usually gathered either at our farm or Grandpa Gilbertson's where the day's hunt would be planned. Back then the corn rows in the corn field were planted farther apart than they are now, and were easier to walk though so we did a lot of corn field hunting then along with sloughs.

The usual participants were Dad, me, Uncle Lyle, Uncle Lowell, my cousin Gary, Walter, and sometimes, Uncle Astor Underthun or Dad's cousin Julien Gilbertson. I never remembered Grandpa Gerhard hunting with us, but I remembered that he had balance problems and that was why. I heard that he used to be a very proficient hunter!

I've been told by my Uncle Lyle and my Uncle Verdie that Grandma Selma only liked to eat hen pheasants because the meat was more tender but the hunting laws were changed to make it illegal to shoot them! I pheasant hunted a year or two before I finally shot down my first one. It's a trial and error thing and took time to learn to lead the pheasant.

I used to go hunting on my own a lot too and walk in the fence rows between fields and other farms was always good for a pheasant or two. I would do that either in or out of season! Ha! One method I used was to hunt alongside the corn picker when Dad was picking corn and what I would do was to walk about six or ten rows out from the corn picker and watch ahead for a pheasant running down the corn rows away from the picker. Then I would either "ground swat" them or attempt to shoot them when they flew. Either way I did pretty well!

Another method I used would be to shoot them at night out of the trees in our grove. I would use the .22 rifle for that, but right after sundown when there still was a little light in the night sky, I would load up the rifle and creep quietly through the trees out to the north edge of our grove and look up in the tree branches and sometimes see pheasants roosting for the night. If I could get close enough without spooking them, I would sight down the side of the rifle barrel and fire. Sometimes I got one, sometimes not, but I only got one shot that way as the survivors would immediately fly off! This was, of course, out of season also!

One of my favorite times spent with Dad was during the fall duck hunting season, at least I think it was the legal season! Anyway, towards evening Dad would say "let's go get some ducks for supper", so he would grab the single shot 20 gauge and a few shells and off we would go to a pothole south of us on Joe Lynne's farm. It was surrounded by corn so we would hide in the corn rows waiting for whatever type of duck would fly in.

It wouldn't be long before either mallards or pintails or even the smaller teal would come in to land on the water. With Dad, it was usually two shots and two ducks and off we went back home to clean them for supper. I was too young then to shoot the shotgun so Dad did the shooting. No doubt I had to wade in and retrieve the doomed ducks in the middle of the pothole but can't recall that part.

Occasionally a flock of Blue Geese or Snow Geese landed in the south field to feed during their migrations. Sometimes if Dad got close enough he shot down one or two before they flew off. It was very rare to see Canadian Geese then as their migratory pattern was further west. Now days there are so many of them and being so pesty, they are otherwise known as "flying carp."

There were lots of pocket gophers on the fields and sides of our driveway and I would spend a great part of the summer trapping them. They always stayed underground and would push the dirt from their tunnels out causing the numerous dirt mounds in somewhat of a pattern. A mound had to be searched for the tunnel entry and then that had to be made large enough for a trap to be set in it. Then small branches or corn stalks were placed high enough over the trap so as not to spring it. Then the whole thing had to be covered back over with dirt.

The traps had a chain and that had to be staked down so the trapped gopher couldn't drag it off. When a gopher was found in the trap it was usually dispatched and fed to the cats. Sometimes if I waited too long to check the traps and a gopher had been in the trap too long, it would chew through whatever leg was caught and be long gone with a paw left in the trap!

One time I found one that had just been caught but not really injured much so I put it in the basket on my bike and headed home with it still in the trap. I managed to get it out of the trap out in the lawn and it immediately started digging a hole and could it ever dig fast. In only a minute or two it was already down a foot and so I pulled it out of the hole by putting a stick down there which the gopher would bite long enough for me to pull it out. Then it would start digging in another spot and the process would be repeated again. It was great fun watching it "destroy" our lawn cause when it dug, the dirt flew out all over, then it would stop and push some out with its front paws.

This went on for a while up until Dad came home from the field and saw what the gopher had done. He was not happy! So I had to shoot the gopher in the hole and fill it in along with all the others on the lawn. What we wouldn't think of for entertainment. In the spring the striped gophers would be out in the road ditches and that was even more fun because we would hunt them with .22 caliber rifles, and try to hit them from far away.

Hunting them was somewhat of a springtime ritual because on Sunday afternoons the country roads were well occupied with cars loaded with people just driving around looking for gophers to shoot. After I got my driver's license and some years later my friends or Cousin Gary and I would do that same thing ourselves and have competitions on who could shoot the most or the longest shot!

One particular type of bird that was seldom seen on our farm was the blue jay. I was out in the woods one day and saw a blue jay feasting itself in a robin's nest! I immediately got the shotgun and started blowing away blue jays and after that anytime I heard one I would go hunting for it. So it wasn't long before the sight of one was a rare event.

An event I always looked forward to in the winter months was the Mandt-Jevnaker sponsored fox hunts. The bounty on them back then was around $30.00 per fox and was good revenue for the two churches as each hunt would bag anywhere from 20 to 35 fox.

Notices would go out and anywhere from 150-250 or more hunters from all over would show up at Mandt Church where we would load up into the beds of covered farm trucks and head out to a previously determined hunting area. The hunt would take place on four square miles of farmlands and would work like this. Starting at each corner of the mile square sections a hunter would get out of the truck about 200 yards or so from the 1st guy, with the spacing determined by how many hunters there were. When the last ones were dropped off, the drivers would then drive around again giving the start signal. Then we would all start walking toward the center point of the four square miles with the goal of trapping fox in the ring.

The walking conditions were determined by the snow conditions so each hunt was different. Sometimes it would only take an hour to meet at the center, sometimes twice that long.

On one hunt over by Denny Skogrand's farm the snow was fairly deep in one spot but crusted over so we could walk on it without breaking through but several deer were spooked by us hunters and ran out into this snow and had broken through with their small, sharp hooves and couldn't get out fast enough. We were able to walk right up to them and touch them! They just stood in that deep snow and were just shuddering and shaking with fear of us! Back then, deer were a pretty rare sight in our area.

With the usual four farm homesteads per square mile, we would still walk straight through the farm yard, waving at someone in the house or even to greet them! No one minded someone walking through their property back then! Try it now!

As the "ring" tightened up and got smaller, shots would start ringing out when a fox was sighted, or sometimes when another critter was seen. Before my time during these hunts, jackrabbits were also bagged along with fox because there were so many of them but as their numbers declined they were off limits but on every hunt there were always some "jerks" who would shoot them anyway and just leave them where they shot them! I even watched guys shooting owls and hawks!

I never was fortunate myself to shoot a fox on these hunts although on time a fox came out of some hiding place and was running parallel to me about 20 yards away. I was carrying the 20 gauge single shot and was so excited at this perfect opportunity that I missed over and behind! By the time I reloaded he was gone down the line and was being shot at and "missed" by a bunch of other hunters till he disappeared. I guess we all had "fox fever".

Because of the eventual close proximity to other hunters the only ammunition allowed was bird shot and shotguns. Buckshot was not allowed although I know some guys used it.

On one hunt, and at its conclusion, someone had dragged a wounded fox up on the gravel road and a circle of guys were standing around it when some "dip shit" pulled out a small automatic pistol and shot it in the head. With the road being frozen the bullet went ricocheting off with a "whine" and luckily didn't hit anyone!

Dad, being one of the hunt organizers was standing nearby and immediately got in his face and demanded the pistol! I had only seen Dad that pissed off a few times and could see that he would have got physical with the dumbass if he wouldn't have obeyed. The guy realized real quick that Dad was serious and gave it up! Dad gave it back to him at the end of the day but we never saw that guy again!

The hunt ended when all or most of the fox at the center were shot, with the exception of one or two hiding in the culvert under the road intersection. There were then several shooters designated to shoot them as they were driven out from the other end for safety reasons but it never played out that way because lots of others wanted to shoot also so when a fox came running out it was usually shot up so bad by so many shooters that the pelt was no good!

We usually had two hunts a day a couple times during the winter months and then would all gather at the church for lunch and hot drinks put on by the Ladies Aid. A good day was had by all.

Chapter 8

Hanson's Grove

My main hangout away from our farm was Hanson's Grove which was about a quarter mile west southwest and across the main gravel road. It was my "escape" place when I needed to either get out of something at home or just for a change of scenery or just to hunt rabbits someplace different.

There were quite a few apple trees there along the road with several different varieties of apples so it was a very popular place in the summer time. And the township also used the clearing in the middle of the grove to store gravel for use on the township roads so there was always a big gravel pile to climb.

Wild strawberries also grew in the north side of the grove and when they were in season I would spend hours hunting for them. What a treat!

Obviously we weren't the only visitors to Hanson's Grove as there were usually fresh tire tracks in and out of there and occasionally we would find a stash of beer hidden back in the trees by who knows! The full bottles would make great targets for a BB gun, and one time Joey Lynne and I found a full case and proceeded to empty them all out and put them back where we found them! I don't think that we ever found any more after that!

Other nocturnal visitors to the grove had different things in mind as over the years we would find evidence of their presence in the form of semi-transparent soft rubbery tube shaped items that were discarded from the back seat of a car! In my younger years these things were sort of a mystery to me but as I got older and being a farm boy around farm animals and cattle being inseminated by the veterinarian, I finally put it together! And in my later teenage years and knowing who lived in the surrounding neighborhood, I had my personal suspicions of who the donors and recipients probably were! There couldn't have been a more perfect place in the whole area other than parked behind the gravel pile in Hanson's Grove to "do it".

Chapter 9

Visiting

A major activity and a main part of our farm culture was evening visits with neighbors and relatives and it was mostly farm families that did it, with few exceptions. There were two questions asked depending on the time of year. "Are the mosquitoes bad over there?" Or "Can we get up your driveway?"

The main families that we visited and were visited by were my uncles and aunts Lowell and Mildred Armstrong (Dad's sister), Astor and Vernice Underthun (Dad's sister), Grandpa & Grandma Gilbertson, and Joe and Sidonia Lynne (neighbors) and once in a while Verdie and Agnes Gilbertson (Dad's brother) and when we went over to Grandpa & Grandma Gilbertson's, Lyle and Rudy, who lived on the same farm place would walk over to visit if they were home. So those were always fun times to get together with the cousins too.

In most cases these visits were instigated by me or my brothers just to hang out with the cousins and we would beg and beg Mom & Dad so that eventually the phone call would be made and off we would go for an evening of play. And then the evening would end with a big "lunch" with coffee and Kool-Aid and all were happy!

About once a year we would go up to St. Paul to spend a couple days with Humphrey and Elizabeth Paulson (Mom's sister) and their kids Terry, Cindy, Jimmy and Charlotte. That was a whole new experience for us kids, from the farm to the big city. What a treat to ride bikes on sidewalks and paved streets and where I also got a quick introduction to big city "gang turf" as we were chased after if we wandered too close to certain neighborhoods and challenged to a fight!

One time when visiting at Armstrong's' lunch was being served along with the required coffee for the grownups. Well, this time the coffee Mildred had percolated in the coffee pot looked funny and smelled funny as it was green instead of brown! It tasted so bad that she had to pour it out wondering what was wrong with it. After dumping the grounds out, out came a soggy package of hair dye that my cousin Sharon had hidden in the bottom of the pot. Mildred & Lowell were pretty mad and embarrassed but all was well after a new pot was brewed and that incident provided many a laugh for many years after.

In the springtime it was sometimes a real challenge just to get up Armstrong's driveway as Lowell never graveled it so it was all mud after the spring thaw. We had to get a good run at it at a higher than normal speed just to not get stuck in a deep hole halfway up the quarter mile driveway. Even after that we had to all wear rubber overshoes to get from the car to the house.

The times of extended family closeness and togetherness pretty much came to an end with the passing of my dad's generation. When I was a young boy there weren't many family reunions like nowadays because we regularly got together with the "rellies" for birthdays and picnics, etc. That was still the era when people just didn't move far away from their family. On Dad's side, all my aunts & uncles lived within a 12 mile radius except for one uncle.

Chapter 10

Grandparents

Grandpa and Grandma Gilbertson

Grandpa and Grandma Gilbertson on their 50ᵗʰ Wedding Anniversary. They were married for 74 years.

Gerhard and Selma Gilbertson were the grandparents that I saw the most and spent more time with as they lived just three miles away. That being said, they, of course, were taken for granted as young kids usually do with anyone who is "older"! But they were very unique in their own way and I hope I can do them justice with my attempts to put on paper a few descriptions that are flattering to them and that others will recognize about them.

Grandpa was around six feet tall and lean and lanky and big boned with a full head of hair. He was afflicted with a balance problem in later years and when he walked we called it "high stepping" as he would raise his legs higher than normal. And he would grab onto furniture or church pews or anything in range to help him maintain his balance.

Some of my earliest memories of him were when we visited them and always, at some course of the night, us kids would get up in his lap or huddle around his chair, ever mindful of his "spit can," to have Norwegian stories be told to us. The two main stories he told us I can only remember vaguely but one was about a young boy who was stolen by an eagle and was carried up to its nest on a mountain top and somehow he escaped, and the other one was about a boy or man who was being chased by wolves across a frozen lake and crawled under an overturned canoe and chopped off the wolves' paws as they were clawing at him. I guess I should ask my cousins what they remember of those stories. He sure captivated us kids with them.

Grandpa Gerhard also chewed "snooz" and there was always a newspaper laid out with his coffee can "spit can" in the center of the paper, the paper was in case he missed the can! I never knew him to smoke anything but he was never without his "snooz". When I was older I drove out to pick him up for a day of fishing. I always kept my cars spotless. We were driving over by Kerkhoven to some fishing spot on the river when he rolled down the window and let go of this large mouthful of snooz spit, part of which the wind blew into the back seat and the rest strung out on the side of my car all the way to the tail light. Of course he didn't think anything of it but I was not happy! At least it didn't stain the paint. I remember it as if it was yesterday!

Grandpa was a hardcore fisherman and would go fishing at any opportunity and so was my uncle Lyle. It was not unusual to drive out to Lake Lac qui Parle in the winter and see them out on the ice and fishing from their car. Grandpa even had his own minnow tank. I don't think that there was a lake within a 50 mile radius that I didn't fish at with Grandpa, with probably everyone's favorite lake being Lobster Lake north of Starbuck. Dad even told lots of stories about fishing there when he was a kid.

Grandpa Gerhard also had a talent for inventing things. With one of his inventions he applied for, and was issued an official United States patent in December of 1957. You can look it up in Google patents, then type in Gerhard Gilbertson. It was a toy that he made for kids to play with and it had a spring loaded plunger with a cup on the end which shot a ball high up in the air when another ball was thrown at the actuating lever at the bottom of the body of it. I remember playing with it with the cousins at family gatherings.

It's also been said that he had come up with the basic idea and design for an open faced fishing reel when he was younger, but that he couldn't figure out the mechanism that rewound the line back and forth evenly on the reel. Someone else beat him to it. Wouldn't that have been a patent to hold!

In the later stages of Grampa's life his memory started to leave him. In 1979 after I had returned from a three year assignment to Germany, Dad and I drove out to see him and Gramma. I couldn't wait after not seeing them for three whole years. When we walked in the house Gramma was so happy and excited but Grampa just sat in his chair and stared at me and he didn't know who I was. That was so heartbreaking. Dad was even surprised that Grampa's memory of me was gone. Dad kept trying to get him to remember me but it was futile. He still talked some to Dad but not to me. I would still go out there to see them when I was home from Grand Forks, but it was always the same. Not long after that Grampa had to go to a nursing home in Appleton and passed away in 1984. He was 95. To this day I still miss him.

Gramma Selma was a little over five feet tall and not fat or skinny. Just right for a Gramma! When she said my name, it always was with two syllables "Al-len" with the first syllable a low tone and the second half a high tone! And I can still hear her say my name that way.

I never knew her to be in any other mood than a good one although she could snap at Grampa occasionally. Of course they could both do that pretty good too. One night we were over there having lunch and Grampa was telling us about something and Gramma kept interrupting him saying "No Pa, that's not how it was," or something on those lines. Anyway she interrupted one too many times and Grampa was fed up by this time so he said very loudly to her "Ya, ya, you tell it then." It got pretty quiet all of a sudden while Grampa cooled down and she giggled nervously and found something else to talk about. Mom & Dad and all of us had a good laugh over that for many years.

On the subject of lunch, Gramma's specialty was salmon sandwiches and it was a rare event to have something other than salmon. And she always pronounced salmon literally as it is spelled, emphasizing the letter "L". I guess that probably comes from her first language of Norwegian. The letter J is pronounced as Y and vice-versa, and this is one thing that made Gramma unique. When she made lemon (yellow) Jell-o, she didn't call it "yellow Jell-o". To her it was "jellow yello" and it being said with a heavy Norwegian accent!

"Rubber necking" was one of Gramma's favorite pastimes and anyone back then who was on a telephone party line knows what that means! Most if not all rural telephone systems were party lines which were coded with multiple subscribers with each phone having a different ring code, i.e. one long, two long, one short, two short and so on, and everyone knew all the other rings because everyone's phone on that line would ring no matter who got called!

On Grampa & Gramma's phone line there were probably four other homes in the area and Gramma knew each one's ring tone. We would be over there sitting around the kitchen table eating lunch again, and the phone would ring for a neighbor. Gramma knew right away who was being called and she would fidget for a short time, then couldn't stand it anymore so would go and pick it up with her hand over the mouthpiece and stand in the hallway listening in, or "rubber necking." The caller and called person could hear other phones being picked up as the other customers listened in on what they are talking about. There really was no such thing as a private conversation on the phone. Our phone was also on a party line so it was the same with us! I doubt Gramma ever missed a call, because she seemed to know everything about anyone out there.

Another of Gramma's specialties was growing flowers and that she had an abundance of. She always had hollyhocks and dahlias and other various varieties growing in beds all along the fence around the house and along the house itself.

When us kids were sick with some malady or whatever and were home from school, over would come Grampa and Gramma with a big bottle or two of 7-up for us and it always seemed to make us feel better. Maybe it could have been just seeing them made the difference too. It was very rare that we didn't see them at least once a week at either our place or theirs and we always saw them in church on Sunday. They never missed that.

After Grampa died, Gramma still lived on the farm for several more years until her age, physical condition and Uncle Lyle's inability to care for her because of his physical condition, required a higher level of care and so she had to be moved to Luther Haven nursing home in Montevideo.

She never could accept being there and it was so stressful to go and visit her when we came home for a visit. She would hold my hand constantly and cry and want so bad for someone to take her "home". When we finally had to leave we all had tears in our eyes. I was always depressed about that for a while after each visit with her.

Gramma Selma passed away on the 27th of November in 1989 at the age of 96 and her funeral was out at Mandt Church several days later. It was bitterly cold that day (below zero) and some of the family wanted to postpone the graveside burial service because of it, but Dad made the decision to put her to rest that day so it was done and no one suffered the worst for it. I still make a point of visiting their graves occasionally to say Hi, and to visit the graves of the other ancestors and relatives buried there. That has always been important to me.

One item of note was that Gramma was five months pregnant with Clarice when she and Grampa Gerhart were married in December of 1910. It was never talked about but that went on about as much then as it does now days.

Another little tidbit about Grandpa and Grandma Gilbertson and also my uncles and some neighbors was that when they didn't want us kids to hear a certain conversation they would switch to speaking Norwegian, knowing that we didn't understand it, and then chuckling about it while giving us sly looks!

Grampa and Gramma Weckhorst

*With Gramma and Grampa Weckhorst and Mom,
Ronnie, Lynn and me with my "barn door" open.*

My mom's parents were Carl and Emma Weckhorst and they lived on a farm by Louisburg for a while and then on a farm by Bellingham and they were members of the Louisburg Lutheran Church in Louisburg. The cemetery just west of the town is where they and many of my ancestors on Mom's side are buried.

Grampa Carl had emigrated from Norway as a young man and after he met and married Emma Skordahl they settled near Cutbank, Montana, where my mom was born. After several years there, they moved to Minnesota and settled near Appleton where my mom grew up and graduated from Appleton High School in 1939.

Grampa Carl had a bad leg and limped as long as I can remember. He had a severe injury to it when he was a young man and more than likely never went to a doctor to get it to heal right.

When I was young I would spend a week with them in the summer and Grampa and go fishing several times at the river where we would catch lots of bullheads. He was very good at skinning and cleaning them and taught me how to do it too. Gramma would fry them in flour and butter and they were very good eating.

I had to sleep upstairs in their house and it scared the crap out of me. For years I would have bad dreams about the creepy stairway going up there. They had wood ticks up there too, or maybe they rode up there on me but at night before I fell asleep. I would be picking them off when they were crawling on me.

Gramma Emma was an excellent cook and it seemed she was always in the kitchen cooking or baking something. Her specialties, at least to me were lefse, flatbread, cream bread and beef roasts. She had a rather quiet disposition but always had a smile on her face and had a pretty good sense of humor. She doted on us kids too where Grampa was more standoffish. She also made wine from river grapes and there always was a gallon jug of it that she probably attempted to hide but we always found it and snuck swigs from! My brother Lynn still makes it occasionally using her recipe. Good stuff!

Gramma always wore dresses and in the summer time if she was outside and had to "go", she would hike her dress up a little and pee standing up. Damndest thing I ever saw, ha! She would just bend forward slightly and let it go, smiling and giggling the whole time and of course, it would even run down her leg but she didn't seem to mind! It sure was funny to see.

Gramma Emma died in May of 1962 at only 72 years of age. She and Grampa were at our farm spending the night and I remember being woke up in the early morning to loud noises and lights on in the room where Grampa and Gramma were sleeping. The ambulance was outside and the EMTs were working on Gramma and getting her loaded up on a gurney to take her into Montevideo. She was coughing and trying to catch her breath and it was really scary to us kids. She had a massive heart attack (coronary thrombosis) and died a short time later in the Montevideo Hospital. It was a terrible time for us all.

Grampa Carl stayed on the farm by Bellingham about ten more years after she died and then moved in with Mom and Dad for about 15 years until his health and blindness required a higher level of care.

He then was a resident of Luther Haven Nursing Home until his death in 1986 at the age of 97.

Christmas 1961 with Gramma and Grampa Weckhorst.
Lynn and Ronnie in front. Nancy and me in back.

Chapter 11

Julebokkers, or Christmas fools

The Norwegian word julebokk translates to "Christmas fool" in English and almost every time us and some of the aunts & uncles and families visited at Grampa & Gramma Gilbertson's on an evening between Christmas and New Year's we would get a visit from julebokkers. This was a Norwegian custom and was a group of neighbors or other relatives that would dress up in various costumes of old clothes, coats and masks or bed sheets with eye holes cut out and would park down the road out of sight and come whooping and hollering up to the house and knocking on windows and doors and shouting "julebokk" in unfamiliar voices so as not to be recognized.

This group would then all come in the house and talk funny and tease us to try and guess who they were. If they were dressed and concealed real well and we had no idea who they could be, they would slowly drop hints until the first real identity was discovered. Then usually the rest of them were identified soon after. After the fun and excitement had died down, then they were treated to some lunch or snacks and then off they would go to hopefully surprise another gathering in the neighborhood.

Julebokking was always done between Christmas and New Year's as was the custom and it seemed that every family had boxes of old clothes from which to make up crazy costumes to wear. Some people wore used nylon hosiery over their head but it was a little easier to recognize features under them.

Dad's cousin Julien Gilbertson and his wife Cora and son Gary, my second cousin and my age, were part of the main group of Julebokkers and whenever they heard of a holiday gathering of people they knew in the neighborhood, off they went, all dressed up and ready for treats!

One night we were home and it was later in the evening and almost bedtime when we saw several flashlights moving around out in the yard and then some loud knocking on the door and windows and we knew the "fools" had arrived! Mom hurried to get the coffee & lunch started as 6 of them filed in and started the usual funny voice talk and teasing about stuff they knew about us.

Neither Dad or Mom or us kids had any idea who they might be and all our guesses were wrong and they kept teasing us so finally when the coffee & lunch was ready, they started unmasking and it was the Kvistero family from a couple miles away and good friends of ours. They were Peter and Gunhild and their children Orlan, Keith, Marie and Linda. They were good and had us totally fooled! The longer it took though, the more fun it was. We also went out as julebokkers too but usually only one evening during that week.

Today, Julebokking is almost unheard of and the last time we did it or saw it was in the 1960s. It really was great fun and we all looked forward to that week in the year. Nowadays if it were done they would probably get shot at or have the law called on them!

Chapter 12

Mandt Church

Mandt Lutheran Church

I grew up in a church going family and the church was a half mile north of Grampa and Gramma Gilbertson's farm and two and a quarter miles west of our farm. Besides the church being the main entity to encourage us boys to walk the "straight and narrow," it also was why we had to take the dreaded communal Saturday night bath. I can only imagine what it would have smelled like in church if everyone took baths on Sunday night before school the next day instead!

We all progressed up the Sunday school grades until old enough for Luther League and also had to endure and suffer through vacation bible school for two weeks during the summer school vacation. Who wanted to sit in church school during perfect summer days when there was playing to be done and mischief to be gotten into! But we had to go "or else"!

Every year at Christmas our Sunday school put on a program with all the grades having some part in it. And we all had to take turns standing up and saying a "piece", which was a sentence or so of something out of the Bible. As I was so petrified of that part of the program, almost without fail I would develop laryngitis badly enough to where I couldn't talk! So I would be standing up when it was my turn and rasping out words that were unintelligible and obviously no one could understand what I said. This went on through Sunday school and even school through high school! Amazingly though when I was done and the pressure was off, my voice was miraculously restored!

My Sunday school classmates were Barb Lien and Patsy Johnson. Barb was the smart one, Patsy was mentally challenged and I guess I was somewhere in between! A comical thing involving Patsy and myself would take place during our Christmas program when it was our class's turn to stand in front of the congregation to say our Christmas pieces. Patsy wouldn't, or couldn't say hers and when it was my turn she would lean forward in front of me and stare at me while I was attempting to say mine.

I didn't think much of it because I was used to her being the way she was and was too nervous and intent on my own part in this drama but some of the congregation thought it was rather funny or cute so there was some laughing and giggling going on. That even made me more nervous thinking it was directed at me! Mom and Dad would laugh about that on the drive home.

The ultimate goal to strive for in our Sunday school Christmas program was to get selected to play the part of Joseph and Mary in the manger scene and since I was the only boy in my final year of Sunday school, I was Joseph by default! The year before, I was one of the wise men.

When the program came to an end, the presents were passed out (we all drew names) and the obligatory bag of peanuts, Christmas candy and an apple were given to each kid and all went home happy!

Luther League was the next step after Sunday school and we joined that when we started 7th grade. And this was where the Mandt and Jevnaker churches joined to do this together. We met at Pastor Don Ekerstrom's parsonage across the road from Jevnaker Church one evening each week and my confirmation classmates were Rodney Peterson, Kenny Jerve, Larry Myhre, DuWayne Larson, Barb Lien, Gary Gilbertson, Joey Lynne, Jerry Christianson, Galen Rud, David Larson, Rachel Laeger, Joan Nøkleby and myself. We had to study and learn and memorize certain things in the Lutheran liturgy and Bible and then all be quizzed by the minister in front of the church congregation in order to be confirmed into the Lutheran faith. Then we were allowed to take communion, legally!

Confirmation class from Mandt and Jevnaker Churches 1962

Front Row L-R Joan Nøkleby, Rachel Laeger, Rev Ekerstrom, Joey Lynne, Barb Lien

*Back Row **Allen Gilbertson**, Jerry Christenson, Kenny Jerve, Galen Rud, Rodney Peterson, Gary Gilbertson, Larry Myhre, David Larson, DuWayne Larson*

I enjoyed Luther League way more than Sunday school as it was more a rite of passage into the teen years. All the kids in it were in the grades from 7th to 12th grade so there were a lot of us. We usually had one meeting a month at either Mandt or Jevnaker which was like an advanced Sunday school but with lunch afterward.

There were also lots of fun activities too such as a hayride or two in the fall and Christmas caroling at some of the older area farms and at several nursing homes where elderly church members were residents in either Benson or Montevideo.

We all really looked forward to the hayrides as they were the fun event of the year. They usually started out from Jevnaker Church except for one year we all met at Paul Skogrand's farm and left from there. There were from three to four tractors pulling hay racks with bales of straw spread out on them for seats and would hold 15 or 20 kids. At the start of the ride there was the usual scramble to pick who we wanted to ride with but throughout the approximately two hour ride there was a constant changing of hayracks depending on who wanted to be with who. Of course if we had any interest in certain girls that were on the ride we would hang close to them to either flirt with or tease or just to stare at longingly! If the girl of interest didn't go to our church, lots of hints and cajoling of their girlfriends that did, would go on to get them invited along!

Every so often on the ride a couple hayracks would get alongside each other for a straw fight for several minutes and by the end of the ride there wasn't much straw left. Then back to the church for a good lunch and to pick straw out of our hair and clothes while we ate.

We also went on the annual Luther League bus trip out to the Black Hills in South Dakota and would stay in campgrounds for three or four nights. This fun time would start out with loading up the bus (we always used Simon Olson's bus service out of Montevideo, and he always drove) at Jevnaker Church with the tents and food (we were totally self-sufficient) and then our suitcases and off we went for the half day drive to get there.

We always camped first in a campground above Sylvan Lake and from there we could walk or run down through the pine trees to the swimming beach when we weren't out seeing other sights. The other sights being Mount Rushmore, Harney Peak, Wind or Mammoth Cave and the Black Hills Passion play by Spearfish.

Our camp site was set up with boys in one or two tents and girls in one or two tents and also for the chaperones and was chaos at first until all were situated. We made all our own meals too which was mainly sandwiches during the day and hotdogs or something else warm for supper. Apple butter sandwiches were always one of my favorites.

I can't remember who the chaperones were each year because they were usually different each year but one who went along every time was my Dad's cousin Julien Gilbertson. We all really liked him because he enjoyed being around us and he always played a big part in making the trip fun.

The one thing he did without fail and took great joy in was the morning wake-up greeting of "O.K. boys, drop your cocks and grab your socks." ha! Then off he went chuckling, to the next tent. But never loud enough for the girls to hear!

On one of the days we would load up and go to Harney Peak which was a medium sized mountain with a winding road going up to the top where there was a ranger station. It was about a three or four mile climb one way. The goal was for everyone to walk to the top and back but only a few of us did that as it was sort of a competition to be the first one to the top.

On another day we went up to Mount Rushmore where we spent another half day and early evening to watch the huge spotlights turn on after dark to illuminate the presidents. That was really impressive. Then it was back again to the campsite for evening snacks and to sit around the campfire and sing "Kumbaya" along with other suitable church campfire songs.

Our next destination was a campground by Spearfish so down came the tents and everything loaded back in the bus for the short trip there. This campground had a small mountain stream running through the middle of it so it made for some extra challenges and opportunities for trouble! It seemed that someone always got wet somehow!

From there we loaded up one evening to attend the *Passion Play* which was held in an outdoor theater using real people and animals. It was an interesting production held at night in the very cool mountain air so was a relief for it to end and get back to a nice warm campfire.

On March 7th in 1964 our Luther League went on a three week bus trip out to Washington, DC via Detroit, Michigan where we attended a Luther League conference for several days. Our bus load consisted of senior high school aged kids, our minister Don Ekerstrom, chaperones, including my dad and the bus driver Simon Olson.

On our way from Detroit to Washington, DC we camped at various campgrounds along the way similar to how we camped in the Black Hills. We toured the Gettysburg battlefield site for most of a day and was that ever impressive. After arriving in DC we stayed in a motel on the outskirts of the city for four nights while seeing the sights of our Capitol.

The main sights we toured were the White House, the Washington Memorial, where some of us had to race each other to the top via the thirty or so flights of stairs. Then we went to the Jefferson Memorial, the Lincoln Memorial and Arlington National Cemetery where we visited the grave of President John F. Kennedy who had been assassinated less than six months earlier. I remember that while at Arlington walking among some of the more famous person's grave sites, I had read stories and books about them and viewed them as somewhat fictional, mystical characters and here I was at their actual resting places. Wow, they were real living people after all! How humbling that was. We also spent about half a day at the Smithsonian Museum but that should have been a couple days as it was so big.

The day we toured the US Capitol Building, we got to meet with Senator Hubert H. Humphrey and Congressman Alec G. Olson who represented our district back home. What an amazing and impressive place that was. To actually stand on the spot where Presidents Lincoln and Kennedy lie in state after their deaths was very humbling. We also took a boat ride on the Potomac River down to Mount Vernon to tour George Washington's home.

During one of our last nights there, we all were victims of a crime. What happened was we went to the Capitol to attend an outdoor concert by the US Marine Corps band on the big lawn in front of the Capitol. It was really nice and attended by several thousand people at least. Since it was at night, most of us left our cameras in the bus and when we got back to the bus when the concert was over, the front door was wide open and most everything of course was ransacked and most of our cameras were stolen. We went to a police station and filed a report but never saw them again. As it was, not many pictures exist of most of our trip out there.

On our return trip from Washington, DC we visited Harper's Ferry and camped not far from there. We also attended a church service in a very small church way back off the beaten path and sang several hymns in front of the small congregation. We sure were the center of attention there as it appeared that those people weren't used to "outsiders".

Several other items of interest regarding Mandt Church were that there was no indoor toilet back then so the outhouse down by the cemetery was a side by side with boys/men in the right side and girls/women in the left. This made for the perfect opportunity for young boys to "spy" on girls but of course this never really happened because every "peephole" either made or discovered was immediately found and plugged from the other side, and besides that the girls learned to never go in there if they suspected boys were lurking about!

One Sunday as church services were over and we were filing out, several fairly large chunks of plaster from the ceiling in front of the balcony came loose and fell down and one chunk hit my aunt Vernice on her shoulder. She wasn't hurt bad enough to be hospitalized but could have been far worse had it hit her head. Mandt Church was rebuilt in 1909 but it was mostly cement made with river sand and plaster and was deteriorating rather quickly and that incident was just one of others. The church was eventually demolished in 2002. The church bell is the only part of the church left on the site and is on display on a roofed over pedestal and when we have the descendants of Jens & Sarah Gilbertson reunions at the home farm, my uncle Verdie makes several trips up there with a hay rack full of kids so they can all take turns ringing the bell.

As a further testament to my "brattyness," my cousin Gary and I made the church registry records one Sunday. We were early teens at the time and old enough where we didn't have to sit with parents as that was not cool, so we sat up in the balcony during the service. Being "shitheads" we would "crack" our ankles during the sermon when the service was at its quietest. Those rather loud pops would echo loudly and we would sit up there snickering while people would look up and glare at us occasionally.

One Sunday the minister, Don Ekerstrom, had enough and stopped his sermon and shouted up at Gary and I to come down and sit with our parents. How embarrassing that was and more so for Mom and Dad as I was in trouble for a long time after that. Many years later, during the final service before demolition, there was lots of reminiscing about the earlier years and the current minister read some excerpts from the record book and that incident was one of them! As soon as he finished reading that part, half the people there, all around my age, were looking at me and giggling about it. They hadn't forgotten it either, after all those years!

Another item of note was that every Sunday before we left for church and Sunday school Mom would put either a pork, beef or ham roast in the oven, cooking while we were gone and ready to eat when we got home. How great it was to walk in the house hungry and smell a good meal ready to eat.

More on my confirmation class, and this was rather odd and humorous! Barb Lien and myself were the confirmants from Mandt Church and in the church bulletin the Sunday her and I were confirmed it listed Barb as the valedictorian and then me! That title was only used in public school for the top graduate and we had no grades in confirmation class so that was odd but then because of my neighborhood reputation it was most likely a stab at me from the church "do-gooders" who put the bulletin together. Using that reasoning, I should have been the salutatorian which was awarded to the 2nd best student! *Note: Barb and I had a good laugh about that at the funeral for Tim Haugen in Montevideo on 12-12-11.*

Confirmation at Mandt Lutheran Church. Barb Lien, Rev. Ekerstrom and me.

When Mom's Aunt Ida came to occasionally spend a weekend with us and go to church with us even I would be totally embarrassed by her! When she was younger she was a choir member of some big church in Minneapolis and so thought that she was a world-class soprano. So when a hymn was being sung she would erupt into a high-pitched off-key wail louder than anyone else and this, of course, brought stares and laughter from the congregation!

Chapter 13

Our Cars

The first car I remember us having was a black 1951 Ford. Dad also had an old pickup truck up till when I was about six years old but can barely remember it. Dad kept the 1951 Ford into the early 1960s when he finally retired it out in the grove behind the shed. He had bought a 1960 Dodge in about 1960 so it must have been new or just barely used. And when he started selling grain seed part time he bought a used 1956 Plymouth Savoy and this was what I mostly drove through high school until I enlisted in the Air Force.

Being a farm boy, Dad started me driving early. First the tractor and then the 1951 Ford which was great for me but also a help to him with various farming activities. And later I got a farm permit and then my real driver's license at 15. A year earlier than town kids so that was something to flaunt!

Dad's main rule for my driving before I got my license was that I could only drive on gravel roads - no highways! So sometimes I just forgot! Of course any excuse to drive that I could dream up I took advantage of. Since some of our farming equipment was shared with Grampa Gilbertson and Uncle Lyle and Dad needed something from over there, off I went, any reason to drive.

I became more mobile with the ability to drive and the more experience I had, the more Dad let me go. So any chance I got, I was hunting, staying at Gary Armstrong's or over hanging out with Randy Stay.

When I started to spend a lot of time in Montevideo and when I was dating the one thing I was fanatical about was never driving a dirty car. I even went so far as to carry a half full water pail and stop to wash off the dust that had collected on the wheels during the mile and a half drive from our farm to the highway. Most all teenagers were that way back then. We just took a lot of pride in what we drove.

One "no-no" I did one night on the way home from Montevideo was when I intentionally ran over a skunk on the gravel road about a mile from home. I knew better, but…! I had driven the 1960 Dodge family car that night and when I hit the skunk it sprayed from the front bumper to the rear as it was tumbling under the car! I knew it was bad, as the smell even on the inside was overpowering and what was worse was that I parked it in the garage. Dad was pissed! He woke me up the next morning for a good ass-chewing and all my excuses that it was an accident fell on deaf ears. That car must have stunk for at least a month before the skunk spray finally wore off and people could even smell it coming out of church! Anyway, after that I avoided skunks at all costs.

I really didn't see myself as being a "wild" one. I was given certain liberties as a teen by parents who were fair enough to reward hard work by giving those liberties and not keeping a tight leash on me. As long as I didn't overstep what I was allowed to do things were fine.

Dad was more lenient. He never talked much about his teen years but I understand he didn't have a lot of restrictions on him either in his day. If we were of the same era I believe we would have been good friends to hang out with!

Chapter 14

Family Trips: Up North and Out West

On the road going up North. Eight of us all fit in the car. L-R,
Mom, Nancy, me, Ronnie, Lynn (looking at his Smartphone)
Gramma Weckhorst and Grampa Weckhorst.

Allen, Ronnie, Lynn and Nancy at Lake Superior near Duluth, Minnesota

Most every summer on the farm we all would take about a week's trip up north to various lakes where we would stay in resort cabins, usually a different one each night. Itasca State Park and Lake Superior were always included and with stops in between. The amazing thing about these trips was the number of people that squeezed into the car. There was Mom, Dad, Nancy, me, Lynn, Ronnie, and Grampa and Gramma Weckhorst all in Grampa's 1957 Plymouth! And one year my cousin Mary Skordahl came along! We managed but it was a good thing that we didn't have to drive very far each day. Back then it seemed that about every lake had at least one resort with cabins to rent so there was never a problem to find something. No reservations were needed either. If the first choice was full then the next choice was nearby and had a cabin to rent.

When visiting Itasca State Park we always did the "walk across the Mississippi River", and like most "Minnesotans" I've been across it numerous times. Two years ago (2009) I was camping with my grandson Teagan near Itasca on Long Lost Lake, and he crossed it for his first time and was thrilled to do it! It just has not changed in all those years.

We also went to the Black Hills in South Dakota on a couple of trips. While there we always went to Mount Rushmore and to Deadwood to the museums and the graves of Wild Bill Hickok and Calamity Jane and all the various "tourist" shops, and just driving around and enjoying the mountain scenery. One resort we stayed at was at the base of a small mountain full of pine trees and easy for us boys to run around and climb on. Dad asked the resort owner if it was all right for us to be up there and if there were any rattlesnakes there and was assured that yes, we could be up there, and no, there were no rattlesnakes in the area.

Well, that proved to not be true as when my brothers and I were running around and climbing rocks and just exploring, I ran to a downed pine tree and jumped on top of it and leaped off the other side. Just as I leaped off I heard this strange rattling sound and looked down in mid-air and saw this huge rattlesnake coiled up and rattling his tail. I don't think it struck at me or at least I didn't see if it did but had I not jumped over the tree but instead just stepped over it I would have stepped right on the snake. I hollered at Lynn and Ronnie to stay away and to get back to the cabin and I shook for the rest of the day I was so upset. Dad was pissed! Not at me but he sure went and let the owner have it!

After we were in the car and on our way, Dad kept trying to calm me down by telling me what a great trophy I would have if I would have went back and killed it! I guess he was right as the more I thought about it, I did regret later not doing that.

A couple years later we went on a week's camping trip out west to Yellowstone National Park. The reader of this may think that our family obviously was well off enough to afford to get away on trips like we did, but it wasn't the case. According to Dad, in those days it was very hard to borrow money from the bank without good justification but that they (the bank loan office) believed that a bank loan for vacation to just get away was a good investment on their part. The value was in the time away from the daily grind to de-compress and re-charge and return refreshed with a renewed work ethic. That was a loan that was never defaulted on.

I firmly believe that because of Dad's war experiences and the heavy combat he experienced on Saipan and Tinian in WWII that he had the experience of downtime between battles to rest and wind down and that that carried over into the rest of his life.

Chapter 15

Pinworms and other Maladies

I would be very surprised to hear of a farm kid who never had pinworms at least once. We sure had our share of them as it was inevitable that being around cattle, pigs, chickens and dogs and cats and their crap all over the farm place led to our constant exposure to whatever was living in it. Washing hands was sort of a prevention against pinworms and other germs but we were lucky to wash hands probably every other day unless we were playing in the cattle tank!

The first indication that we might have pinworms was a constantly itchy butt and to be more specific, the butt hole! Dad would suspect it right away after seeing us kids walking around and scratching, so off would come our pants for the butt inspection and after viewing the evidence in the form of tiny white worms at the above mentioned area, the diagnosis was confirmed and off we went for the worm killing medicine at Rexall's Drug Store in Montevideo.

I don't think pinworms are as common now as they were back then and I don't remember that we had them every year, but I do know that I had them several times on the farm. It was something we didn't brag about or tell others!

The stomach flu was another common annual illness that we couldn't avoid. Once someone in the community got it then it spread like wildfire. Sometimes all of us had it at the same time so the smell of vomit was thick in the house. I also had the chicken-pox and mumps, but the most serious illness, other than appendicitis at three years old, was when I got hepatitis along with Mom, Lynn and Ronnie. The day

I got sick with was when going along with Dad to the grain elevator in Milan.

They had a pop machine in the office and I wanted one so Dad bought a Dr. Pepper for me which was new at that time and I had never tasted it before. Well, I drank that down and shortly thereafter, I got real sick and was vomiting. That was the start of hepatitis, which is a liver disease. My eyes turned yellow and with no energy I missed three weeks of junior high school. Lynn had it so bad he went into convulsions and had to be hospitalized for several days.

We don't know how we picked it up as it had to come from bad water or food and is very contagious. In fact so contagious that any neighbors and relatives who had been in any contact with us had to go to the doctor for a gamma globulin shot which was only given in a butt cheek. Needless to say, we weren't very popular with them for a while after that, ha! To this day I can hardly drink a Dr. Pepper without going back to that day and cannot donate blood because of it.

As a young kid I had too many teeth on my upper bite so as I was slightly "buck-toothed." Our local dentist, Harry Haugan recommended I have braces to correct the problem. Knowing our history with him, I wonder if it wasn't an ulterior motive of his to inflict further pain on me! If it was, it worked! It was hard for the folks to afford it but off we went to Madison to the orthodontist there. I first had to have teeth pulled to make room for the teeth being pulled back. As painful as that was, it was nothing compared to the pain of getting the braces put on and the pulling process starting. My teeth were so painful that I couldn't chew anything for several days and just the touch of a soup spoon on a tooth was almost unbearable. The braces back then encircled the whole tooth and they were quite the mouthful.

The braces had little hooks on the lower back teeth and on the upper front side and on these hooks went small rubber bands that constantly "pulled" my upper teeth back. I took the bands out to eat and usually would forget to put new ones back on so the folks were constantly telling me to get those bands in! I also was fitted with a head harness to wear while I slept, which had heavier duty bands for extra pulling. That contraption obviously didn't get used a whole lot.

A main hazard of mouth braces was that any bump to the mouth while playing, wrestling or whatever was instantly painful and bloody. One time during Physical Ed in 7th or 8th grade in Milan, I got hit in the face with a basketball and the force was so hard that the front braces on both upper and lower teeth went all the way through my lips. Of course there was blood all over the gym floor and I was in the locker room trying to unhook my lips from the braces. That hurt worse than getting hit by the basketball.

Overall, I wore those braces for four years. Then a "retainer" on and off for several years after and in the long run I guess it was worth it.

7th Grade

Chapter 16

1960 - To the Big School

7th Grade, Milan, Minnesota

We could only go to country school through the 6th grade and then it was on to junior high school. Our district was now consolidated with the Milan school district where two years before, it was with the Montevideo school district and that was where my sister Nancy went for those two years.

Milan High School was different than other schools around in that all grades from 1st grade through 12th grade were in the same building, with the elementary grades occupying the 2nd floor and 1st & 3rd floors belonging to the high school classes. But it wasn't a huge school as it averaged around 350 students total. There were 52 in my class. The school was the west side of the town of Milan which was a small town with a population of around 300-350 people.

That was also the end of either walking across the fields to country school or Dad driving us on crappy weather days. It was now the hour long bus ride. The bus route would alternate routes every week so we would be either one of the first to be picked up or one of the last. If we happened to miss the bus on the early route then Dad would drive us a mile or two to catch it before it left the area for Milan, but if we missed it on the late pick-up route then it was off to Milan with Dad, and then he was pissed! Later, after I had my driver's license I would occasionally get to drive the 56' Plymouth to school so of course that was always an incentive to "accidentally" miss the bus!

What a rude awakening high school was over country school. Everything was on such a larger scale. Classmates, classrooms, the library, an actual lunch room, a baseball field, a football field and two gymnasiums with real hardwood floors! It sure was a great feeling to dribble a basketball on the basketball court and actually have it bounce straight back, unlike the dirt area we had in country school where I never knew which direction the ball would bounce!

I was really passionate about basketball even though I really sucked at it! Trying to play it on a country school dirt court did not lend much to basketball talent and experience like what most of my classmates had that went through grade school and playing on the high school courts. Of course I thought I was better than I really was and proceeded to join the 7th grade team where we would get to play against other school 7th graders. I was pretty much an end of the bench warmer! This went on through 9th grade before I finally figured out that I would never make the varsity "B" squad so I quit.

7TH AND 8TH GRADE SQUAD

*Milan Junior High Teams 1961. Look for me
in the front row second from right.*

*1ˢᵗ row. L-R Charlie Kashmark, Joey Lynne, Doug Bertness, Galen
Rud, Jerry Christianson, **Allen Gilbertson**, Rodney Peterson*

*2ⁿᵈ Row. L-R Dale Spray, Bob Miller, Gary Larson, Daryl
Dvergsten, Mickey Thorsland, Dave Moe, Delmont Molden*

*3ʳᵈ Row. L-R John Lundgren, Doug Spray, Richard
Bakken, Pete Roiland, Lowell Haff, Doug Johnson*

We played one game over in Ortonville and we were either way ahead or way behind so I got put in to play guard. So I'm dribbling the ball just past the center court line when somebody started hollering "shoot, shoot!" Well, I got too excited over hearing that so I heaved the ball as hard as I could and it miraculously swished through the rim for two points, nothing but net! There were no three point baskets then.

It was pretty amazing to make a basket from near the center court at my size and age, but what wasn't amazing was that I was immediately pulled out of the game by our coach Mr. Bud Johnson, and put back on the end of the bench and that was the last time I ever got to play in a game.

This probably went on in most school athletics; the inevitable hazing or "initiation," as they called it, of the new underclassmen would occur and it happened to the 7th graders after our first basketball practice. We had heard through the grapevine that it would happen and were scared to take showers after practice was over. Sure enough, just as we filed into the locker room one of the seniors, I won't mention his name, on the varsity was waiting for us with a jar of analgesics, which was used to heat up sore and stiff muscles and joints.

He ordered us to undress and get in line! He stopped in front of each one of us and told us to take a scoop of "grease" and reach down "there" and rub it on the "sack". The term was called "greasing" and "shit", "shit", "shit", did it ever burn. It hurt even worse than being hit down there! Then we had to take a shower that even made it worse.

We may have had tears in our eyes but we didn't dare cry. Getting dressed wasn't easy either as any touch was instant agony. The victims were me, Joey Lynne, Jerry Christianson, Galen Rud and Rodney Pederson. Whoever's Dad that picked us up for the trip home asked us what that strong smell was! Even though it was winter we were all in the car and sweating terribly form the extra "heat" and for some hours after getting home.

I played the trombone in band after begging and begging Mom and Dad for one and because other neighborhood kids did the same to their parents! That was obviously something that the folks couldn't afford because they had already bought a clarinet for Nancy, but they finally relented. I was blessed with a band instrument that I sucked at even worse than basketball. I had absolutely no talent for it and always sat in the last chair of the trombone players. I tried out for the marching band also and lasted through 7th grade until I was cut from that and in order to stay in the band was convinced into being one of the banner carriers marching in front of the band. In fact I finally quit that after 9th grade and dropped band altogether.

I also sang in the choir until 10th or 11th grade until I got the "boot" from that after not seeing eye to eye with the choir director, Bud Johnson! I believe there was a pattern there! Throughout my participation in basketball, band and choir I always had issues with him as he was either in charge or the coach of all those activities. We obviously didn't like each other so getting away from him was the best thing for me. The "boot" from choir happened on the day the Milan Senior Choir sang on Channel 7 KCMT in Alexandria, Minnesota. Most local schools took part in doing that around Christmas.

After our performance, we had a lunch at one of the local Alexandria restaurants that had room for all of us. I was at a table with several other choir members and made a stupid decision to pull a new prank I had learned from someone, I can't remember who but anyway I put a table napkin over a full glass of water, pulled it tight and quickly turned it upside down on the table. As the napkin got saturated I tore it loose from around the rim so it now looked like just an upside down glass on the table.

Well the waitress came by to clean up our table, grabbed the glass and all the water spilled out on the table! She was pissed! It just so happened that Bud Johnson was standing there and he was pissed too! So ended my singing career. I was still very behind in the "maturity" department.

To go along with that, I was not a very good student overall. I loved physical education class and was excellent at most of that, other than basketball! But most of my other classes were average at best. I guess if it didn't interest me I wouldn't give it my all. Probably my favorite classroom class was history, an interest of which I still have to this day. Second was English that was taught by Mrs. Johnson, Bud's wife! Imagine that! I always did pretty well in that class partly because I liked Mrs. Johnson and because I was such an avid reader of library books. I really understood sentence structure even though I had a problem naming each part of a sentence. Along with that I always excelled at reading comprehension and would usually finish first in a timed reading test with the best or near best comprehension score.

Reading was my passion throughout my school years. I know I read most of the books in our country school library and pretty much spend most of my non-class time at Milan H.S. in the school library. Our study hall was connected to the library so instead of the studying I should have been doing, I was in the library! So many books, so little time!

At home when I had homework to do I usually had a library book to read hidden inside a school book so the folks would think I was really studying or doing my homework. I just couldn't see the value of homework when there was a story to be read. In the summer months when school was out a Bookmobile from the Montevideo library would make rounds in the rural areas and it would stop at our country school for an hour every other week. I never missed it and would always check out anywhere from five to ten books and return them two weeks later for another armload! Reading was definitely my priority.

Wearing "long johns" in the winter was standard dress for farm kids and not much thought was given to it until we started high school. We pretty much wore them most of the time at home because of cold drafty houses. They sure felt good when standing at the end of the driveway waiting for the school bus and the cold ride to Milan. The embarrassing part came the first time I had long underwear on and had to undress and put gym clothes on in the locker room. There the teasing by the "town" kids started, but what could we do? The folks insisted on me wearing them on real cold days so on went the teasing. Eventually I got out of having to wear them to school after complaining about it being too warm in class.

Basketball was the sport I was most interested in but I also went out for football mainly because most of my friends did, and I pretty much sucked at that too. For one thing I wasn't as big as most of the others on the junior high team and I wasn't very physical in that I would avoid physical contact if at all possible! And this problem came to light with the coach right away even before we got our so called uniforms.

On uniform day of course I got put at the end of the line and since all the good stuff was already taken I was stuck with a cracked helmet! A freakin cracked football helmet! Needless to say the writing was pretty much on the wall for my football career, but the end came a few days later. Oh, by the way, before that, we had one game against another school and I never got to play a down!

At that time I had teeth braces and before we could practice we had to have fitted mouth guards. These were upper tooth guards that also acted as a cushion against the lower teeth. These guards had a malleable substance that softened up when put in boiling water and so we stood in line to have them put in our mouth and then had to bite down to force our teeth into this extremely hot clay like substance and then let it harden to form fit around our teeth.

Well, I had braces so this procedure didn't work very well and even thought it was adequate enough for the playing time I would never get, the coach finally told me while I was dressing for practice that since I had braces I couldn't be covered by the school's insurance so therefore I couldn't be in football and needed to turn in my uniform AND THE CRACKED FREAKIN HELMET!! Oh, and to go along with all that, the football cleats I was issued were not the same size!

One sport I did excel at was cross country. This was a new sport to our school and the first season was started in my junior year. What led up to my success in this sport was our school bus route. When the bus got to the Lynne farm which was on highway 40 a mile and a half south of us, on alternating weeks it would either turn left and we would be let off first or it would turn right to circle around and then we would be the last ones off the bus. On the weeks that it turned right I would get off the bus and run all the way to our farm to beat the bus before it came around to our driveway. I didn't realize it then but that race with the bus conditioned me to be able to run long distances.

Our race course went east of the football field and through the Opjordan farm and then out around a corn field then back through the Opjordan farm around the football field and then up the hill behind the baseball field to the finish line. The course length was 1 and 8/10 miles.

Our first cross country race in Milan was against Ortonville. They had a fast starter who would set the pace in the race later for their main runner who would then outlast their opponents who would tire out trying to catch the fast starter. Well, the race started and sure enough the fast starter took the lead and we were told by our coach Mr. Solbrack to let him go and catch up later in the race, but I wasn't having none of that!

They were on our turf and were not going to control the race so I went after him even though my teammates were telling me to slow down and pace myself. I caught him about a quarter mile into the race at which point he virtually quit and then I decided that there was no way their main guy was going to catch me. I was in the lead the rest of the race and even though my teammate Bobby Miller almost caught me at the finish I came in FIRST. Yea, I won the first Milan High School cross country race!

Mr. Toussaint, who was the coach told me I would be his main long distance runner in the mile race when the track season started but that never panned out. I did O.K. but the longer distance was my specialty. That one race though was the last one I ever won and even though I did well in other races I never equaled that first Milan H.S. cross country race. I doubt that there was any school records or history about our first cross country season! I never found any. My senior year I was a cross country captain but suffered a back injury in the early part of the season and never ran at school again.

Of note was the fact that we were first issued track shoes but since they had spikes made for sprint races, we elected to run barefooted and sometimes would put duct tape on our feet for some protection. In the fall time during cross country, the golf courses we usually ran on were either very cold or frozen so the tape really helped. There were no specialized running shoes then like the hundreds of styles now. We either had track spikes or regular high or low top tennis shoes and those were too heavy for track or cross-country.

High school sporting events were a big part of our school days and in my first years in Milan I never missed a home football or basketball game and even went to some of the away games. Mom and Dad would occasionally go to a game but if I didn't get a ride with one of the neighbors then they would drop me off in Milan on their way to Montevideo for Friday night shopping and then sometimes pick me up on the way home. The community ride to and from games was alive and well and whoever drove would many times have a car full of neighbor kids to either pick up or drop off.

After most home games there would be a dance downtown in the American Legion Hall and it was always packed with school kids from about 9th grade on up. The music was naturally rock n' roll and played on a record player with small 45 rpm records. Since there was no real disc jockey there was a sort of pecking order as to who picked what songs to play, with girls mostly playing the fast dancing songs and boys picking the slow dance songs, understandably! The opportunity to slow dance with a girl that I had a severe crush on was both intoxicating and nerve racking at the same time and of course being a somewhat normal guy with raging hormones I couldn't dance too close and risk the possibility of showing how I really felt! Guys had it tough dealing with that problem!

One of our neighbor farm girls, Leone Nelson, first taught me how to fast dance enough where I wouldn't make a complete fool out of myself. She was three years older and a very good rock-n-roll dancer and I was so appreciative that she would take it upon herself to help me out. I danced with her a lot until her boyfriend showed up after dressing from a game and then I was on my own.

Although I really liked a couple girls in the class below me I never dated anyone from Milan H.S. In my sophomore year I met Kay from Montevideo who was a year younger than me and we went together throughout high school and beyond. In 1968 when in Thailand, I received a "Dear John" letter from her and that was pretty much the end of us. We got back together for a while a couple years later but it just didn't work out.

Lime vodka, ugh! That was the culprit the first time I experienced drinking alcohol when I was a junior in high school. To this day I still remember the taste of it when I see it on a liquor store shelf! On the occasion of a football game between Milan and Appleton at Appleton, Demore, Doug, Lyle, and myself managed to get someone older to buy for us a pint of lime vodka. There was a park just northeast of Appleton that we drove to for some privacy and where we kept daring one another to take their turn in draining the bottle. It went down easier by plugging the nose when swallowing! The desired effect was soon attained and not long after that the vomiting started and where I first learned to feel better faster by sticking a finger down my throat!

After this our stomachs felt better but we were definitely under the influence and off we went to the football game! We hung out near one of the end zones so that others, especially adults wouldn't smell the alcohol on our breath and we were trying to stay balanced while attempting to sit on a wood railing. About that time one of our teachers, Mr. Schilling, came walking by giving us a suspicious look. About that same time I lost my balance and fell backwards to the ground. Of course he stopped and asked "Have you boys been drinking?" Our immediate replies were "No, Mr. Schilling, not us!" He just eyed us suspiciously for a moment and then walked off! He knew! Sometime later we did it again only we tried orange vodka and the end result was no different and we got drunk and sick again. It sure was good that alcohol tasted so bad.

The night before our senior class trip to Chicago by train out of Montevideo, I spent the night at Demore's home. We managed to get a pint of cherry sloe gin so we sat up in his bedroom and mixed the gin with 7-up and wow, did that go down good. It was almost like drinking Kool-Aid and of course the desired effect was attained! We sure were drunk and since we had to be at the train depot real early in the morning we were still really high when we got there. If the chaperones would have found out about us we would have been prevented from going on the trip so some of our classmates were busy keeping Demore and I away from them. Once we were underway the hangover eventually started and I slept it off during half of the trip to Chicago!

I managed to stay trouble free during our stay in Chicago and hung out mostly with Colin and his cousin Cindy and just had fun. One of my roommates got caught drinking by the chaperones and was pretty much relegated to staying in the room unless we were off doing class stuff.

Demore and I sometimes stayed out all night on a school night but we had to fool our parents to do it. I would ask Mom and Dad if I could stay overnight at Demore's home and he would do the same. After school was out we hung out in Milan until there was nothing else going on there, and then on to Montevideo or Dawson. We had a mutual friend in Dawson that would hang out with us at the pool hall till he had to be home and then we just drove around. After curfew we stayed out of Montevideo because if the police caught us they would call the folks.

The fun would soon wear off though and around two or three a.m. we were tired and bored and trying to think of what else we could do! Eventually we would end up parking in the small town park in Milan waiting for school to start and then struggle through a day of classes with little or no sleep.

The most memorable event that happened while in high school was the day President Kennedy was shot. I was sitting in 10th grade Industrial Arts class when word of it was passed to each classroom over the loudspeaker system. At first we all were wondering if it was some sort of joke because it just couldn't be. There were a few snickers and someone in the class said "right between the trees."

A note on why this was said! The current hot T.V. show was a new comedy hour called *Rowan and Martin's Laugh-In* and we all watched it religiously. It was on Thursday night and one of the skits was about one of the main characters on a swing between two trees with various punch lines that proclaimed "right between the trees". Of course the next day at school in the hallways between classes this phrase was widely used as we were already very influenced by television.

Anyway there was a lot of giggling over that after it was said but it soon turned silent as the reality of what happened set in. Then it wasn't funny anymore. I still remember who said it. As we sat there stunned another announcement came over the loudspeaker that President Kennedy had died and we were to be dismissed from school and to wait for the buses.

As we went to our lockers the hallways were full of crying teachers and lots of crying students and it was such an awful scene. The bus ride home was almost total silence except for the younger kids and when I got home Mom was crying and Dad would tear up too.

Since it was Friday and shopping night in Montevideo off we went to sell eggs and pick up the milk check and grocery shop. It was a very somber scene in Monte too. Hardly anyone was talking and there were lots of tears flowing and stunned looks with most people on the sidewalks. During the next four days all television programming was preempted for coverage of the assassination and funeral. Grampa and Grandma Gilbertson didn't have a television so they came over to watch the funeral. I was real obsessed with the whole event and only left the T.V. to eat or sleep. Our comfortable world had just changed!

MILAN PUBLIC SCHOOL
MILAN, MINNESOTA

STUDENT IDENTIFICATION

1965-1966

NAME   Allen Gilbertson

Student ID card

The spring before graduation we had our senior class counseling session with the principal Mr. Peterson and when it was my turn my history teacher Mr. Schilling also sat in. Mr. Peterson asked me what my plans were after graduation and I told him I wasn't sure but maybe college! He then basically told me to forget about that because of my grades (my GPA was near the bottom of my class) and that I should consider the military because I had a lot of growing up to do! Imagine that! Mr. Schilling told me the same and that I should consider the Air Force because he did an enlistment and liked it. I never had any plans for college anyway and don't know why I even said that. Maybe because so many other classmates were.

Graduation from Milan, Minnesota High School in 1966

I knew I didn't want to farm the rest of my life, so I guess the seed was then planted. Also at that time we were visited by the various military recruiters so I took more of an interest in the possibility of joining up. I knew that there was a good possibility that I would be drafted for Vietnam and of course I wanted to join the Marines just like Dad did so I could kill bad guys, but Dad told me no way in hell was I going in the Marines! I actually listened to him!

The main social event in Montevideo during my high school years was "dragging Main" on weekend nights. Those of us who had cars or parents' cars would make the circuit from the north to the south end of Main Street continuously for several hours while also waving to the other "draggers" every time we would pass. Since Main Street was about a quarter mile from one end to the other, greeting the same driver went on repetitively throughout the evening. The turnaround point at the north end was by the creamery (no longer there) and the turnaround on the south end was over the railroad tracks and by the bowling alley and the Holiday gas station. And if a car with guys would meet a carful of girls and wanted to talk to them they would point down to the back alley running parallel to Main Street to meet and flirt or even exchange riders!

Dad got to checking the mileage when I took the car and I would get a good butt-chewing if it came back with lots of miles on it. It didn't take long before I figured out how to unhook the speedometer cable from under the dashboard after I had put the requisite miles on the car. I hooked it up again right before I got back home. Of course I forgot to reconnect it one time so it was evident to Dad when he drove it the next day. Another big butt-chewing for me. He finally quit checking it because he never would really know the mileage I drove for sure.

During my senior year in high school, I would occasionally spend a weekend in Mankato where my best friend Randy Stay was in his freshman year at the State college there. The college environment was a whole new experience for me and I loved it. It was pretty much a continuous party during the weekends and we were involved in a lot of it.

Randy and Allen Johnson, also from Benson, were also best friends and roommates in T&C Apartments on the campus. It was technically a dormitory on campus and so there was a desk person who "screened" anything and anyone coming into the building. Since we were underage and there was no alcohol allowed we tried, but couldn't get our beer purchases past the front desk to their room. What worked was to load up a suitcase with a case of beer and pull it up to their room on the 2nd floor by rope! Where there was a will, there was a way!

After getting somewhat drunk, the tackle football game in the living room would start. Furniture would be moved off to the side and each team of four guys would get four downs to get to a designated goal line. It got pretty rough as there were no rules. Finally, after a number of touchdowns and expended energy and beer effects, we got it getting cleaned up and more presentable and then it was off to the Mankato party scene. Randy told me not to let anyone know that I was still in high school so I kept my mouth shut and it was assumed that I was a fellow classmate! It worked.

My sister's soon to be husband, Gary Fonkert, was from Dawson which was about 16 miles west of Montevideo. His brother Terry was my age and, oh boy, was that a whole new world hanging out with him. I thought that I was a little wild and out of control but I think Terry wrote the book on that.

Terry's world revolved around fighting and partying and he excelled at both. He was known in the multi-county area as someone not to mess with and he would demonstrate that fact with exuberance! He lived to fight!

One night I went to Dawson to hang out with him and after tiring of playing pool in one of the Main Street beer joints we got in his car to drive around. Well, here comes a car down Main Street with six guys in it from Madison that Terry recognized. That pissed him off as he knew they were there to look for Dawson girls. So he started following them and exchanging the middle finger and words with them and finally had enough so he decided to stop them. He told me that when we had them cornered that I was to take two of them and he would beat up four!

I had never been in a fist fight in my entire life and was scared to death about the near confrontation. Terry was so nonchalant about it. He couldn't wait and I'm was literally praying to God that they would get away. Well my prayers were answered and they finally got out of town, but that was Terry Fonkert.

Another time, when he came over to Monte to hang out with me, we went out to *Len's Nightclub* that was on the way to Granite Falls. We entered and were walking along the booths against the wall and there sat Billy. He was known as the Montevideo tough guy and him and Terry knew of each other and of course hated each other. Billy said something smart-ass to Terry and before he finished talking, Terry punched him, knocked him out cold, pulled him out of the booth, dragged him to the front door and threw him out on the ground! Then we went on with the rest of our night! You just never knew what would happen next being around him.

In the summer of 1966 I graduated from Milan High School and what a great feeling. No more school! Yeah! Now what? The next significant event was when my sister Nancy got married to Gary Fonkert a week after my graduation in early June.

Chapter 17

A Job in North Dakota

Later that summer a neighbor, Keith Kvistero, who was about five or six years older came over one day wondering if I could go with him up to North Dakota to haul flax straw bales off the fields after the harvest. We would be gone about two weeks and he would pay me $1.00 for every ton of bales that we loaded up, weighed and unloaded at the collection point. That sounded like a pretty good deal and sure beat hauling manure for the neighbors but Dad had to agree to it because he relied on me to do a lot of the chores around the farm. He finally gave in and in a week or so Keith and I were off to Grandin, N.D. which was about 50 miles north of Fargo N.D.

Keith drove their farm truck and pulled a bale trailer and I drove his car. It was about a 300 mile drive making for a long day as the truck and trailer could only do about 45 miles an hour at best.

We rented a bedroom from an older lady in a small town nearby and the next morning, after an early breakfast in the town restaurant, we were off to the fields. Flax straw was in real demand as it was used for rayon and other products but it would soon be supplanted by polyester. The bales themselves were the standard farm sized square bales tied with twine so I was used to handling them.

The real difference was that flax straw is very strong and sharp on the cut ends so a pair of denim blue jeans would only last at best two days before the thigh areas on both legs would wear completely through to the skin, and that really stung. So every other day, and sometimes daily we would head to the local farm supply store for new pants. It was odd to see brand new pants from behind with the front all worn out. We also wore out a number of pairs of leather gloves.

We were told each morning what farm fields to go to after the baling was done. We loaded up the trailer first with me lifting them up on the trailer and Keith stacking them. Then we unhooked that and did the truck next. We averaged about four loads a day. Then we hooked up to the trailer and went off to Grandin to be weighed at the elevator. Then we went out to wherever the collection point was. We dropped the bales into a big elevator that carried them up to the big bale stacks. Then back again for another load.

While up there I had another close call with death! We had finished loading bales on the truck and were starting to hook up to the loaded trailer. Keith was backing the truck while I was holding up the trailer tow bar to hook up to the truck. We had done this many times and had a system down but this one time something went wrong. Either his foot slipped off the clutch or the truck wheels hit a low spot and all of a sudden the truck jumped backwards. Somehow I sensed what was happening and just ducked under the bed of the truck before it slammed into the front of the trailer. It was tons of weight coming together fast and I know I wouldn't have survived it.

Keith thought I was a goner too as he shut the engine off and came running back expecting to see me crushed between the truck and trailer. We were both pretty shook over that and were very careful afterwards.

We had been doing this from sun up to sun down for ten days straight and were starting to get burnt out but we thought we could stick it out for the two weeks. However, on the morning of the 11th day we had just arrived at a new field southwest of Grandin and what we saw right off was the decider for us. The bales were wire ties, which meant that wire was stronger than twine so the bales could be packed tighter by the baler, which translated to heavier bales! After just a couple of bales we looked at each other and said "the hell with this", threw the bales off the trailer and packed everything up. Keith got paid and off we headed, for home.

In that ten day period we had hauled 200 ton of bales so my cut was $200.00 which was, at that time, pretty good pay.

Chapter 18

Joining the Air Force

That summer after several visits with the local Air Force recruiter, Sgt Bob Klatt I had signed up to join the U.S. Air Force. I was then quickly scheduled for the induction physical and AFQT (Air Force Qualification Test) in Minneapolis at the induction center. One fine summer morning off I went to Minneapolis with my girlfriend and two of our friends who were dating. Since it was close to the downtown area they went there while I was being prodded, poked, stuck and tested.

The physical part was done en masse and there were about 40 of us who were going into the various branches of the military. After the obligatory paperwork, we were told to line up in two lines facing each other, then told to strip naked. As if this wasn't embarrassing enough, a doctor, (I hope,) came down the line grabbing us, "down there," and having us turn our heads and cough, and when that was done we had to turn around, bend over and spread our cheeks!

The blood test was next and we lined up in front of a caged window and in it was the biggest black man I'd ever seen. Of course I was really scared and dreading my turn as he was yelling at guys to "stick your hand in farther", "quit pulling your hand back" etc.! When I saw the expressions on the guys before me after they were stuck, I wanted out. But I did my duty and endured what I considered the worst blood test ever as my finger was sore for a week afterward. I was destined to see this same guy again some years later!

After the physical the written tests were next. There was no pass or fail as the test's purpose was to determine what category our aptitudes leaned toward. The four categories were mechanical, electrical, administrative and general. I scored the highest in mechanical so I knew I would be a mechanic in some specialty, just didn't know what yet. We were to find that out once we were in basic training.

Basic Training

Nice new haircut

GILBERTSON
ALLEN O
AF1G975428

Basic training photo at Lackland AFB, Texas 1966

In the fall of 1966 I received the order to report for basic training on December 4th and I was to leave on the bus to Minneapolis the evening before. As the day got closer I was getting more nervous and the fear of leaving home and my family and girlfriend was dominating my every waking moment. I knew my life was about to change and was really torn over wanting to stay in my comfort zone and yet the need to fulfill my obligation to my country. I knew that I couldn't back out of my commitment, but I sure questioned my enlistment decision!

The evening of my last day at home my girlfriend came out to the farm to drive me to the bus stop in Montevideo. As we were saying our goodbyes and Mom was tearing along with me, Dad suddenly walked outside because I know he didn't want us to see him crying! When it was time to get in the car he gave me a hug and immediately turned to walk to the barn and I could tell he was sobbing. I'll never forget seeing him walk away like that. That pretty much set the tone for me the rest of that night.

The drive to town was mostly in silence as I'm sure I wanted to stay strong in front of my girlfriend but when the bus pulled up for me the tears really started to flow and I was so choked up I couldn't even tell her goodbye as I boarded. What an awful moment. What an awful night. I took a seat in the back and waved to her until we were out of sight and then finally confronted my sadness alone. Even forty-six years later almost everything about that night hasn't been forgotten.

The next stop was in Willmar to pick up my enlistment partner, Paul Sjodin. We hadn't met before that night but I knew who he was when he boarded the bus. I avoided him most of that bus ride as I was just too sad to talk to anyone.

Courtesy of the Willmar West Central Tribune

After we got to the hotel in downtown Minneapolis we were given a room each and after a mostly silent phone call to my girlfriend I went to bed and attempted to sleep but then there was a knock on the door and it was Paul. He wanted to know if I was hungry as him because some other inductees were going out to find a place to eat. That was finally the highlight of that day as I was getting really tired of feeling sorry for myself and dearly needed a distraction!

Most of those guys were going to be in my basic training flight so it was great to meet them then. After finding some place to eat and then walking around for a while it was back to the hotel for a few hours of sleep and then up early so as to be at the induction center to be sworn in with the enlistment oath. Then we were off to the airport for the flight to San Antonio, Texas.

When we arrived at the Minneapolis airport we were told to wait until we got our tickets: inside the circle on the granite floor that depicted the world atlas. This circle is still there in front of the ticketing and baggage check-in counters and most of us who have been at the airport know what I'm describing. It's odd to go there occasionally and see it still there and to remember that once I was told to stand in that circle and not to step out until told to do so!

We flew out on Braniff Airlines to Dallas where we were to change planes for the final leg to San Antonio. We had a very long layover between flights so several of us pooled our money to take a taxi down to Dealey Plaza, the site of the Kennedy assassination. It hadn't changed in the three years since and was a very humbling experience. We wandered around downtown Dallas for a couple of hours and then went back to the airport for the next flight.

After we landed in San Antonio, we boarded an Air Force bus for the trip to Lackland AFB, and into "HELL"! No sooner had the bus stopped when a sergeant came onboard and proceeded to scream at us to get our "bleep, bleep, bleepin" asses off the bus and line up." The spit was spraying out of his mouth as he was screaming loudly and there were swear words and references to body parts that I'd never heard before.

Needless to say, we were scared shitless! Being in a state of shock was probably more correct as I was pretty sure there was some underwear that needed changing! We were told after our swearing-in at Minneapolis, to memorize our service number before we got to Lackland, I did that on the plane ride, and I'm glad I did because heaven help those who didn't, or forgot it. The TIs (training instructors) screamed that question at us constantly just looking for a reason to get on us even more.

After our nice welcome we were loaded back up for a midnight breakfast at a chow hall where we endured more screaming and name calling from the barracks that would be our home for the next eight weeks. We then had to each pick a bunk, empty out our pockets and our suitcases so the TIs (two of them) could go through everything to look for anything illegal.

If one of us were to stand out for any reason to a TI, it would usually mean a new name that would stick to that person for the duration of basic training. For instance, one of the black guys had what was called a "French tickler" in his wallet. This item was a special prophylactic for female pleasure and when the TI discovered it then this guy's new name was "Frenchy". He was called this throughout basic. One of us guys from Minnesota had the last name of Fjelsta and he was hence known as "Alphabet". There were others with new names but I managed to stay pretty much unnoticed. They just called me dipshit, dick wad, or Airman Gilbertson! I learned not to stand out.

The first night there was really no sleep as we had lights out at around 2:00 AM and back up at 5:00 AM for a trip to the chow hall. I laid in my bunk and listened to occasional sobbing as we were all pretty much scared out of our wits. I guess I could say I was scared shitless for the first week as it was six days before I had a bowel movement.

After a very quick breakfast we marched to the barber shop where we were all shaved bald and lost what little identity we had left! Then we marched to a warehouse where we were "sort of" fitted for our uniforms and boots and shoes. All this somehow fit in a large duffel bag and off we marched back to the barracks with a stop on the way to purchase soap, toothpaste and shaving stuff. I bought a bar of Dial soap and to this day whenever I smell Dial soap I'm immediately back to that first day in basic training.

When we all had our civilian hair we had formed identities on who was who but after getting shaved bald we all looked different again to each other so we had to re-identify, as we all looked alike! I knew that I had some dandruff but after the shave job it was like a winter snowfall. Some others that had real long hair were really bad with dandruff to the point where they had sores on their scalps. But after several days we all had healed up.

The main goal of basic training is to instill discipline and teamwork and that it did. On the discipline side, we learned, or were severely taught, to do what we were told instantly and without question and what the repercussions would be if not. We were constantly under the microscope! The teamwork side revolved mainly on the marching and physical fitness part of our training. We soon learned that we were now just a number.

Learning to march as a unit was a comedy of errors at first. I had a basic knowledge of it being in the high school marching band but most of these guys had not so it was a real challenge for the TIs. It took weeks for some of the guys to learn the difference between their left and right foot. We were taught to land on our heels with enough force to hear each step and when we did it right and together it made a loud "thud, thud, thud" with each step. We were marching to breakfast one morning when my right boot heel broke off. Since I was too afraid to tell the TI, I just kept on marching.

Finally I couldn't take any more as the nails holding the heel on were now coming through into the boot and into my heel and I could feel the blood. Of course when I announced that I had to stop, I got a good ass chewing and another ass chewing when I showed him my heelless boot, and yet another ass chewing for waiting so long to say something! The ass I had left was getting smaller by the day! After we returned to the barracks I got to wear chukka boots until my combat boot was repaired and since they were way lighter the physical fitness events were easier.

Our flight's two TIs were Technical Sergeant Vincent and Staff Sergeant Pike. It was sort of like the "good cop, bad cop" thing with them as TSgt Vincent was the real jerk and SSgt Pike was more easy going and quieter. He was still hard on us but fair at the same time. TSgt Vincent was a real jerk all the time and we sure hated him. I guess that meant that he did his job right!

There were 43 of us in our training flight. Six of us were from Minnesota and about the same number from Arizona, and the rest were from Florida. Some of the Florida guys were still not accepting the South's defeat in the Civil War as they were constantly calling us Minnesotans "Yanks" so that was a constant annoyance. A few times we almost came to blows because they really got pissed off when we would respond by saying "The South will rise again because shit floats!" They really hated that!

They were raised from generations of contempt for anything or anyone, "Yankee" since the south got its ass kicked in the civil war. So we developed a contempt for them because of such trivial ignorance. They just can't get over it and made any attempt to not let us forget it.

I was a smoker when I started basic training and it sure was a rough two weeks before we were allowed a cigarette. The majority of us were smokers so we always carried our cigarettes with us for when permission to smoke was given. Finally, while standing "at ease" in formation one day the TI said "all right, smoke 'em if you got 'em!" A cigarette never tasted so good, probably also because it was something that reminded us of our previous life! After that first time then smoke breaks became more frequent but we never dared to sneak one without permission.

We had to do a number of extra details throughout basic with KP duty the most infamous! We got stuck with it twice and god how we hated it. We had it once at our chow hall and once at Wilford Hall, which was the big regional military hospital on base. My job there was on pots and pans detail.

On another day we were marched over to Wilford Hall where we were all split up to perform various details in the hospital. Three other guys and I were put on operating room detail where we did cleanup after surgeries were over. I didn't mind that as we were supervised by civilian nurses who didn't yell at us and who also let us watch a caesarian operation.

Barracks details pretty much dominated our time when we weren't out marching or doing other training tasks. Since the floor was a dark burgundy color we had to hand polish it by applying cordovan shoe polish by hand and then buff it with an electric buffer. We learned to never walk down the middle if we could help it but to walk around the sides to get to our bunks. One night the barracks next to us had a fire drill and all of a sudden our back door burst open and all those guys came running into our barracks and on our newly polished floor. Of course it was arranged by our TIs just to piss us off and to have us re-do the floor again. We were constantly tested like that!

Our latrine was all open with about twelve stools and six or eight urinals. One guy was picked to be in charge of it and so he was called the "latrine queen". Everyone had their turns in latrine duty (it sure was fun scrubbing off shit stains with a toothbrush!) but he was the one who got chewed out if it wasn't constantly spotless. Since there were no stalls around the stools that was the main factor with me not having a bowel movement for almost the first week. I had never had to take a dump with someone watching me before and to sit there out in the open with other guys was just too embarrassing for it to work. Finally the dam broke and what a "huge" relief. What worked after that was to put elbows on knees, hands over ears and keep eyes closed! Ha! We were learning fast that any personal privacy was a great luxury.

The first thing to do after being woke up at "0 dark 30" was make our bunks. This was done even before dressing and they had to be tight and perfect or risk being tore apart by a TI to be redone. Foot lockers were perfectly arranged or else. There were a number of times that one was overturned and the contents strewn all over the floor because something inside wasn't perfectly aligned with another item. Our uniforms were hung on clothes racks behind our bunks and there had to be no wrinkles, everything facing the same direction and the hangers the same direction and perfectly spaced. Yes, they would be measured!

Completing the obstacle course was a major basic training milestone and the week before we were marched there for a walkthrough where we were shown the correct way to do each obstacle. The weekend before our test Don Garbet and I were detailed to perform guard patrol at the course with the purpose of keeping kids from base housing from playing there. It was a one day detail and since we were shown how to do the obstacles we had a whole day to practice on each one. On test day it paid off as I was the 3rd fastest through and Garbet was 4th.

Next door to our barracks was a building with a break room where we would occasionally be given liberty to go to. There we could smoke, eat ice cream bars and candy out of vending machines or watch some television, and that was where we got liberty to watch Super Bowl "ONE". That game then was nowhere near the big deal it is now. In fact Super Bowl One was never seen again because the network covering it re-recorded over the tape it made!

The rifle range and marksmanship testing was the final major milestone. Since the M-16 was pretty new to the military it hadn't been approved for basic training use so we were to use the .30 caliber M-1 carbine which was a WWII era rifle. It was a very easy rifle to operate and shoot though and I qualified expert with it. In later years I made several attempts to qualify expert with the M-16 but never shot quite good enough.

Towards the end of basic we had a major inspection of our bunks and uniforms and footlockers with the reward for having no discrepancies being a day pass to San Antonio. About our uniforms; there could be no loose threads, or "cables" in Air Force speak, anywhere, and that included threads around sewn seams. We got to be very adept at using cigarette lighters to burn off anything showing that "had no purpose".

Boots and shoes had to be completely dirt and dust free to include the soles we walked on and to be highly "spit" shined. A spit shine was just that. Using spit along with black Kiwi brand polish to create a mirror shine on the toes of our combat boots, chukka boots and low quarter dress shoes. I used water instead of spit and it seemed to work just fine. It took hours of constant circular fingertip motion with a wet cotton cloth and dabbed with polish to an initial shine. After that it didn't take so long.

We had to stand at attention in front of our bunks where we were "thoroughly" inspected for proper uniform wear and personal hygiene, as in a close shave and no ear wax. The front shirt seam had to be perfectly in line with the belt buckle which had to be perfectly in line with the pants fly. Footlockers were again inspected for underwear and socks folded correctly and basically everything else showing no sign of use! The biggest culprit in the footlocker was the shaving razor and blades and any shaving residue was an instant demerit. I hardly ever used mine as I didn't need to shave every day and when I did I would sneak into the storage room at night and dig my electric shaver out of my stored civilian stuff and use that.

I passed the inspection, along with five other guys, with no discrepancies and got to spend a day in San Antonio as a reward. We had to wear our dress blues though and that sucked but it was a great day all the same. We went to see the Alamo and just wandered around in and out of stores and a restaurant or two until we had to be back at the base. Of course we missed the bus we were supposed to catch, got back late and got a major ass-chewing for it!

As far as a physical change after completing basic training, I was somewhat heavier. The day I started I weighed 129 lbs. and the day I graduated I was 165 lbs.! It was, of course, very physically challenging and we all ate accordingly.

Several days before graduation we were told what our jobs would be for the rest of our Air Force lives and I was to be an Aircraft Armament systems mechanic. In other words a "knuckle dragging" bomb, missile, rocket and ammo loader! They made it sound pretty "romantic" though so I was fine with it because I didn't have a choice. A day or so later I received my orders to report to Lowry AFB in Denver, Colorado for technical school training.

During our last day in basic we had a "Kumbaya" sit down with our TIs and with the training atmosphere pressure off we could finally kick back and have a good laugh at all we had to go through. We all realized that the main goal of basic training was to instill in us discipline and to obey orders without question, and this was met. TSgt Vincent was still a jerk but was trying to come across as "one of the guys"! After all was said and done, he performed his duty by the book and I guess we were all better airmen because of him.

To this day I can picture him perfectly, in my face and chewing me out for some insignificant infraction, at least to me, 47 years later! Oh yeah, the last thing he did to us and what was his final shot, was to march us all to the barbershop the day before we left to get our "going away" shave to the scalp haircut. Most TIs didn't do this to their trainees so they would arrive at their next base with at least some hair showing! We weren't so lucky so I arrived at Lowry AFB shaved bald!

Chapter 19

Lowry AFB, Colorado

I loved Denver. From the first day there until the day I left I loved that city. And what a change it was from basic training. I pretty much again had control over my life unless I was in class or on daily detail duty. I even liked Lowry AFB too. It was off of Colfax Avenue on the east side of Denver.

Now I was assigned to a barracks that had rooms instead of open bay so I had only two roommates. One of them, Larry Roulet, was from Litchfield, MN and we became friends. He was in an earlier class than me so left before I did.

Since it would be several weeks before I was to start school I was put in casual status, which translated to awaiting training, and was made available for any detail base-wide. For several days I was detailed to sort out old WWII cold weather gear that was shipped down from Alaska, then worked in the base commissary in the milk department, and the longest time doing KP duty in the chow hall for a couple of weeks. What a relief it was when I got the notification to start attending class.

There were two schools for my AFSC (Air Force Specialty Code) which was 462XO Aircraft Armament Systems Specialist. The TAC (Tactical Air Command) school was for learning fighter aircraft armament systems and the SAC (Strategic Air Command) school was for bomber aircraft, namely the B-52. I was assigned to the TAC course and was glad for it as fighter aircraft were more exciting to me. My class had the morning session which meant our class time was 0600 to 1200 and then to dinner and then off to perform various details around the base the rest of the afternoon.

The aircraft we would be instructed on were the F-100, the F-105, and the newer F-4 but before we had any on-aircraft classes we had to learn the basics of electronics, the Technical Order System, and the various weapons and ammunition that they all used. After those systems were learned and tested on successfully it was on to the real fighters themselves.

The classroom aircraft were all housed in a large hangar across the base called the "black shack" and where we had to have a security clearance to enter. The first several weeks classes were on the F-100 Super Sabre, the next class was on the F-105 Thunder Chief, and lastly was the F-4 Phantom class. What we were taught on these aircraft was just basic introductory stuff unique to each one as the more advanced training would begin at our permanent base after tech school.

After my arrival at Lowry AFB I could hardly wait to put civilian clothes on again because it had been two months since I last worn them. The day after my arrival and after completing most of the in-processing requirements I finally could get out of a uniform! Well, the excitement was over when I literally could not get my pants on and buttoned! The 36 pounds I had gained in basic settled that issue a so it was off to the BX (Base Exchange) at the first opportunity to buy a shirt and pants that fit. I lost most of that weight gradually so then my new clothes were getting baggy on me!

Even though we were no longer in basic training, we still were required to march to and from our various classes. The classmate that was responsible for marching the class was a "yellow rope". This signified that this person had attended a weeklong class on learning all the marching commands as so was identified by the wearing of a yellow braided rope hanging from the right shoulder around the arm. One of my roommates was a yellow rope for his class and convinced me to be one too, the main benefit being that I wouldn't have to do afternoon details anymore and would have the rest of the day after class to myself.

I applied for the class, was accepted, passed, and was then in charge of marching my classmates. Along with the privilege of being a "rope" went a continuous off-base pass where I could go off-base any time I wanted versus having to request a pass on the weekends. It didn't do me much good though as I only went off-base with my friends who weren't "ropes".

Denver was an incredible city and always has been my favorite one since. Downtown Denver was about six to seven miles from Lowry so that meant taking a bus there and back. It was quite the treat to become a civilian again on the weekends after the two months in basic training.

Downtown Denver was also the scene of my first encounters with the anti-Vietnam War protesters and how cruel they were. Being in the Air Force and having shaved heads made us very visible targets of scorn and it would be the unusual downtown trip where I wasn't screamed at, called names, and gestured at with the middle finger.

By law and under orders, we couldn't respond in kind, but also, by law, it was legal for those people to act like jerks and assholes! Being just out of high school and being very politically naïve I just could not understand that behavior. I grew up surrounded by politeness and respect for others and the desire to serve the country I love that gave me, and those people, the freedoms we have. Little did I know, I would experience worse a couple years later!

When in downtown Denver at night our main hangout was the Baja Club which was on the 2nd floor of an old huge building. It was so big that occasionally there would be several bands playing at the same time. We could legally drink 3.2 beer then so we were pretty well "lubricated" and it was quite the wild partying. After closing time the bus ride back to Lowry was something to avoid if possible, as there were lots of sick guys and the smell of vomit was thick in the air! The outsides of the busses were streaked with it by the time they arrived at the base!

Once in a while some of us would pool our money and rent a car for the weekend and then either explore more of Denver or the Rocky Mountains. Dad, Mom and my brothers once drove to Denver while I was there so I got to spend a weekend with them in the mountains.

Other than two movie theaters on base, the only other entertainment was the Airmen's Club. It was an okay place to go during the week and on some weekends there would be a busload or two of nursing students brought to the club for a dance if there was a band playing. Of course they got picked over early according to looks and then it was the haves versus the have nots and naturally occasional fighting would ensue. The Air Police would be called to settle the matter!

The nursing students were about the only girls in Denver that accepted our short military hair, but image is everything so it was pretty hilarious what a lot of guys would do to try to get their hair to grow out faster! The most popular attempt was to brush the scalp with a woman's hairbrush with the belief that it would "stimulate" the hair to grow faster! The BX was always out of hairbrushes. Another attempt would be to constantly pull on the hair with fingers. Who was to say whether they worked or not but it was not unusual to see someone, or a group, walking around, or sitting in a movie theater constantly pulling on their hair! Be that as it may, when I finally graduated and went home on my first leave, I still had short hair.

Chapter 20

Eglin AFB, Florida

My first permanent assignment after completing tech school would be the 25th TFS (Tactical Fighter Squadron) in the 33rd TFW (Tactical Fighter Wing) which flew the brand new F-4D Phantom fighter jet. Before I went there though I got to go home on leave for a couple weeks and it was so great to see family and friends again. Even after six months away I expected everything to be the same there. At least that's what I was hoping for and for the most part things were the same, but yet again, different. I guess the difference was in me. I now started to realize that I was becoming a stranger in what was the center of my life and was now on the outside looking in! Even our farm dog, Queenie, forgot me and shied away!

My best friend Randy Stay called and wanted me to come down to Mankato State where he was going to college. He was having a party at the apartment he was in so of course I went, having spent numerous weekends down there with him during my senior year in high school. I got to know a number of his friends then with all the partying we did together but this time, there was a change. My hair still hadn't grown out much so I stood out like a "sore thumb" in the midst of all these college kids that I used to party with and look like and of course that identified me as military among them. I guess they just felt awkward around me so I was kind of avoided!

After finally realizing that I no longer fit in there, I said my goodbyes to Randy and left for home. I was going to spend the night there and be all hung over in the morning, but I didn't want Randy to feel obligated to entertain me all night either. He could tell it was awkward for me too.

The day I had to leave, Dad and Mom took me down to the Minneapolis Airport and after another tearful goodbye I left for Florida with a stopover in New Orleans. I had to switch planes for the flight to Eglin AFB and there were a number of Airmen 3rd Class (1 stripe) waiting for the flight. Up walks this Air Force Major who starts to chew us all out for having our two decorations (ribbons) in the wrong order. At least those of us that had more than one. I had the National Defense ribbon which we all had, but I also had the marksmanship ribbon and of course I had them in the wrong order. He lined us up in front of other travelers and had us put them in the proper order. Asshole!

Since it was not the summer season yet I had to wear my winter Blues when travelling. Winter Blues were of a heavy wool weave and only felt good in cold weather. Well, it was hot in Florida and it was my luck that my duffel bag with all my other clothes and uniforms got lost on the trip to Eglin and it didn't show up for three days! Here I was walking all over the base while being in-processed having to wear this heavy thick wool uniform in the very high heat of Florida and stinking of B.O. terribly! After multiple trips daily to the small passenger terminal across the street from my barracks to ask about my duffel bag, it finally arrived and then I was accepted socially again!

In my room at Eglin AFB, Florida

On one of my first days there, I was sent out to the squadron weapons loading section to meet my supervisor Senior Master Sergeant Jim Fluey, who was also from Minnesota, and my crew chief Staff Sergeant Jim Riley. I was then informed to not come back until all my in-processing was complete and to wait until they contacted me to show up for duty. Well, my new crewmates Bob Dumey, and Steve Wojnar and I did as we were told and since no one contacted us after our in-processing was done, we played! We played for a whole month, on the beaches and learning how to water ski and stuff. I thought, what a great Air Force I joined! Well, we were finally "caught"! After another major ass-chewing, even the excuse of "You said not to come to work until you told us" was no excuse, we then started to earn our pay.

I was to be the number two man on a four man load crew and my primary responsibilities were to perform the cockpit functional checks and to operate the controls on the MJ-1 bomb lift to load the various bombs and missiles to the missile and bomb racks on the F-4D fighter. This fighter jet was new to the Air Force and could carry and employ most weapons in the Air Force inventory to include bombs, cluster bombs, missiles and rockets and a 20 millimeter Gatling gun pod.

We had to train and certify on each one of the approximately 13 weapons so initial training lasted about four-six weeks. After classroom training we then started the actual load training by the squadron lead crew with an initial walkthrough followed by a minimum three practice loads before we could pass certification. There was a different time standard for each weapon and we had to be under that and with no more than three minor errors, to be passed. Once we were completely certified to perform these loads without supervision we then had to return to the load barn once a month to do MPRLs (monthly proficiency requirement loads) where again we were evaluated by the lead crew. This lasted only about two days though, Thank God!

Florida, for me, was all about beaches and we practically lived on the beach at Fort Walton any chance we got. The beaches in that part of Florida had almost pure white sugar sand that almost looked like snow drifts! In fact, many years later I went back to Eglin AFB for a conference and was put up in one of the hotels down in Fort Walton on the beach. After unpacking and getting ready for bed, as I had traveled there from Germany and was totally drained, I called Deb to let her know I got there okay and mentioned that the "snow drifts" were really large outside the beach side window! She said "what snow, you're in Florida." I was so out of it from the flight that I wasn't thinking right and so must have assumed that since there was snow on the ground at home, it was in Florida too!

There was a huge pier on the beach that we hung out at that went several hundred yards out and where we would walk on to hopefully see porpoises or even a shark, which occasionally we would see. Since it was "down south" in Florida too, the Negro beach was on the south side of the pier and the "whites", on the north side. Unbelievable that that still went on down there, but it was the south and a lot of the local residents didn't like any of us "Yankees" either. I guess they never could get past the Civil War. We had two strikes against us too as we not only were Yankees but we were military also.

Our main tasks at work on the flight line were involving our 24 fighters was arming and de-arming since they all carried external fuel tanks on the wings that had to be jettisoned in case of an in-flight emergency. Electrically fired impulse cartridges were used to jettison or release bombs and tanks and these "carts" were larger than a 12 gauge shotgun shell and full of powder and gas pellets that burned extremely hot when fired and produced the gas pressure that forced open the ejector linkage to unlock the bomb rack hooks.

When we were real bored we used to cut these ejector carts open so we could burn the pellets. One day my crewmates and I had arm/ de-arm duty down at the end of the runway when we got the bright idea of emptying out a bunch of carts into a bigger pile and igniting them. And did they ever ignite! There was this huge cloud of smoke from the pellets and soon after, flight line trucks came speeding out to us to see what was on fire. Needless to say, we got major ass-chewings over that little trick!

Training for Vietnam started in earnest after our squadron was given order to deploy to Ubon Royal Thai Air Force Base, Thailand.

There were several other times that I got in trouble too and got pretty close to the top of our 1st shirt's (sergeant's) "shit list"! These were screw-ups such as oversleeping for CQ (change of quarters) duty in the barracks or just forgetting about an extra duty and not showing up. My punishment would be digging crab grass out of the lawn of the orderly room for eight hours a day on the next weekend with a butter knife. I can recall having to do that three times so I wasn't a very stellar airman in my early Air Force days.

Dad and Mom and my brothers came down to visit me once while stationed there and before I was to leave there for Thailand I got a two week leave to go home. On my return trip back to Eglin I had a layover in the Atlanta airport. When I got off the plane there was a sort of mass confusion and upset people throughout the terminal as word was spreading that Martin Luther King had just been shot and even though there were mostly "us whites" in the terminal, someone told to me to stay in the terminal and told me not to go in the bathroom alone!

The best part of the reassignment to South East Asia was that we all went as a unit so we all knew each other which made the transition easier. I remember very little of the departure other than the confusion of head counts and baggage control and since we left at night it was all so eerie boarding the C-141 transport aircraft with no windows and sitting in web seats facing the rear of the plane!

Our first stop was in Anchorage, Alaska for a short layover, then on to Yokota, Japan for another layover for about four hours, the next stop being our final destination. This was our home for a year! Our total flight time from Florida to Thailand was 26 hours in the air.

Chapter 21

Ubon Royal Thai Air Base, Thailand

On the flight line at Ubon

Allen Gilbertson Is Stationed At Ubon, Thailand

Air Force Sgt. Allen Gilbertson is stationed at Ubon, Thailand, where he is an instructor in weapons standardization and training with the Eighth Tactical Fighter Wing. A graduate of Milan high school, he entered the air force in December, 1967. He is the son of Mr. and Mrs. Roy S. Gilbertson, Rt. 2, Montevideo. His address: Box 4931, AF 169 75428, APO San Francisco, Calif. 96304.

Clipping Courtesy of the Montevideo American-News Montevideo, Minnesota

Upon final touchdown at Ubon RTAB, there was a collective cheer by all but whether it was because we were finally involved in the war or because we were finally done with that damned aircraft cannot be remembered. I do remember the incredible heat that enveloped us when the rear ramp was opened and the oppressively different smells that will never be forgotten. It soon became that we were in a jungle type environment and in a war zone with the continual roar of F-4 fighters launching on a mission or returning from one.

After being bused to our new barracks and picking our bunks and unloading our duffel bags in lockers we were off to the Airmen's Club and some now legal "refreshments" as there was no drinking age limitation there. Ha! After struggling through in-processing with a hangover the next day and getting somewhat fitted with new jungle fatigues and boots, it was off to the flight line revetment area and the shop we would be working out of.

Since our F-4s wouldn't arrive yet for several more weeks we were tasked with storing and stacking all our support items such as missile launchers, pylons, bomb racks and have ready for immediate use; said items, once our jets arrived for the initial weapons loading and commencement of combat missions. Needless to say, it was so hectic a time that we worked 12 hours a day for 30 straight days. There was not much extra time for any partying during that first month.

The Airmen's Club was the main hangout as it had cheap drinks, like 10 cent mixed drinks and five cents beer! The food they had was better than the chow hall too! Since it never closed, there would be a happy hour starting at 6:00 AM for the night shift!

There was a class VI store in the club that was basically an off-sale store where we bought liquor to take to the bars and nightclubs in downtown Ubon. This was also a pretty good bargain as a quart of Jim Beam bourbon was only a dollar! Even cheaper was a quart of Popov vodka that was 90 cents! What was funny about this was that when the booze shipments were delayed and inventory was running out about the only choice left was 100 Pipers Scotch whiskey that no one liked but didn't have any other choice. The only other option was purchasing a cheap bottle of Thai whiskey called Mekong, that was probably just days old. No one bought beer off base but the beer drinkers could drink the Thai beer called Singha. It really wasn't too bad.

Pre loading 500 lb. bombs on a B-52 for delivery to Vietnam

A common weapons load at Ubon AFB, Thailand.

Doing cockpit checks in an F-4 at Ubon.

The night clubs in downtown Ubon were the main draw as they had live bands made up of Thais and most of them were pretty good at playing top American rock-n-roll songs. The Corsair Club was the favorite with the guys I hung out with and it probably held around 200 or more GIs every night. We brought our own liquor from the base and would buy set-ups to mix it with. The bathroom in the Corsair was male/female friendly. In other words, it was not unusual to wait for a bargirl to finish her business while being next in line! And there were no stall walls either. The so-called toilet was actually a porcelain coated hole in the floor with foot pads on the side for squatting over and was flushed by pouring a pan of water down it! Crude but efficient. They were affectionately called "bomb sites"!

With Steve Wojnar in downtown Ubon, Thailand

At my desk as a weapons trainer at Ubon. Plenty of checklists on the wall for the various weapons on the F-4s.

On the day our jets arrived there was an arrival ceremony on the flight line with military dignitaries and then we finally started to do what we had trained so long for. Our crews were split into two 12 hour shifts and my crew had night shift from 7pm to 7am. The day shift crew's main tasking was to assist in launching the jets on their attack missions by pulling all the safety pins at the EOR (end of runway), "safeing" them when they landed from their missions and then removing the MERs (multiple ejection racks) and TERs (triple ejection racks) from the wing pylons and preparing them for the night shift to upload munitions for the next day's missions. They also uploaded the FRAG order munitions on the returning jets for the 2nd go missions of the day.

Night shift was mainly tasked with the FRAG order for the next day's missions and each of us load crews would be given 4 to 5 jets to test and upload the required munitions. Each of our F-4s always flew with 2 AIM-7 radar guided missiles and then a variation of the MK-82 snake eye 500 lb. bombs, M-117 750 lb. bombs, CBU-30s (cluster bomb units), 2.75 inch rocket pods, and occasionally SUU-41 pods that dispensed antipersonnel bomblets, and SUU-42 flare and sensor dispensers. One notable fact was that most of the M-117 750 lb. bombs were WW2 era bombs!

It was pretty much continual mass organized confusion on the flight line 24 hours a day. The jets were parked in reinforced revetments which was three sided protection from explosions and each of the 4 squadrons consisted of 24 F-4s. The first tasks when arriving for our shift was to get our roll-around tool boxes, fill our jungle fatigue pants pockets with ejector cartridges and get the best of the bomb lift trucks (jammers) if we could. This usually meant that our number four man, Bob Dumey, the jammer driver, had to get to work earlier to get his favorite one!

There were two to three munitions trailers full of either MK-82 500 lb. bombs, M-117 750 lbs., CBU-30s full of 700 lbs. of antipersonnel bomblets, or preloaded MERs or TERs. We liked the preloads as they took way less time to hang on the jet versus loading the bombs one at a time. The preloads also had the nose fuses already installed so that we didn't have to string the arming wire to the fuses.

Usually our only break in the action was to go for midnight breakfast at the chow hall and any other down time would be to sleep, read or mess with rice bugs! These bugs were thick over there and the bright flight line lights really attracted them. They were about three inches long, heavy with fermented rice and were to be avoided when driving a jammer. Some guys would glue one down to a table on its back and then put another one on top and they would fight for hours. They had a hooked beak or proboscis or whatever it was called, that was about a quarter inch long and it would gouge out a deep cut. The Thais would eat them because of the rice inside them. They considered it a delicacy. Some guys would catch them by the bag-full and take them off base to sell for one Baht apiece, 5 cents in our money! I even watched Thai security guards on base eat them raw by breaking the head off and sucking the rice out! They knew it grossed us out.

The monsoon season in Southeast Asia was quite the experience. I had never endured constant rain like that and it went on steady for near two months! To work in it was a real challenge. At first we would wear rain ponchos but we soon found out that because of the heat and humidity we would be just as wet under the poncho. We soon discarded that and just performed our work in jungle fatigue pants and jungle boots and even though it was illegal, sometimes wore shower clogs! It was no fun being thoroughly soaked for twelve straight hours.

One night we were tasked to change the weapons configurations from one jet to another and I went and got another jammer to help move the bombs to the other jet. It was raining so hard that visibility was near zero. I was transporting a fully fused CBU-30 full of antipersonnel bomblets and as I turned the corner of the aircraft revetment a truck was heading right for me and I immediately spun the steering wheel to avoid hitting it and since the jammer was rear-wheel steering it threw me off. I never let go of the steering wheel though and was dragging alongside the jammer but not able yet to get back on because of the speed! Holy shit!

The jammer was approaching the revetment wall fast and with a 750 lb. live fused weapon! I finally got back in the seat as the jammer slowed enough and got it stopped just before impacting the wall. Luckily the only harm done was to my jungle boots and my sense of invulnerability!

The monsoon season also played havoc with our uniforms and civvies too as our house boys brought them to their homes to be laundered. During the constant rain for almost two months, the clothes had to be dried over wood fires and did they ever stink of wood smoke when they brought them back! Many times they came back still damp.

About the only remembrance of the chow hall was the incredible heat in there. The cooks behind the serving line were constantly drenched in sweat and it would just flow off their chins and into whatever they were spooning on our plates. We got used to it. It was just extra "salt"! Ice cream was supposed to be a real treat but since the dishes were so hot it was nothing but cream by the time we could eat it.

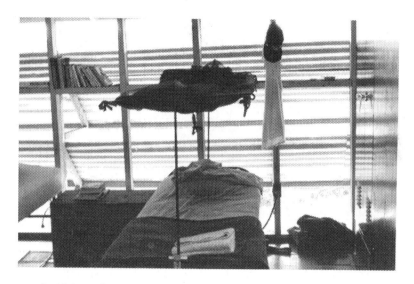

My bunk in "The Hooch" at Ubon with mosquito netting over my head.

Because of the threat of malaria in a jungle environment we were supposed to take daily malaria pills but after initially getting sick from them most of us quit. One day my crew and I were out at the end of the runway arming and de-arming our jets when one guy off the other crew with us started moaning and sweating profusely. All of a sudden he announced that he needed a toilet and toilet paper and with shit streaming out his pants legs he started running up to the flight line! We didn't see him the rest of the day, and that's why I wouldn't take the daily pills! The guys up at our shop were still laughing about him when our shift ended.

Promotion day at Ubon. I went from Airman 1ˢᵗ Class to Buck Sergeant

About halfway through our yearlong assignment our crew was selected above about 80 other load crews in the 8ᵗʰ TAC fighter wing to be the loading standardization crew in charge of all weapons related procedures and training. We were then transferred out of the 25ᵗʰ TFS and assigned to the 8ᵗʰ TAC Fighter Wing. Our new duties were to monitor and evaluate the load crews of the four fighter squadrons to ensure their correct adherence to safety procedures and performance of their weapons loading procedures. After all, we were constantly surrounded by possible "death" and even the slightest mistake could kill someone or multiple someones!

As an example, one of our load crew members in our squadron was so nervous working with all the bombs and missiles on the flight line that he was finally reassigned to a unit that was tasked to transport and upload antipersonnel weapons canisters onto C-130 aircraft. The weaponry in the canister was called Black Spot and instantly armed upon hard contact with the ground and then any further movement would cause them to explode! He was carrying a canister somewhere and he accidentally dropped it, so we were told. He then picked it back up and when it got waist high the canister blew up and literally blew him to pieces! He was told that if it dropped or bumped hard to never touch it and to get away immediately but obviously forgot. There were others there killed and wounded and the call for blood donors came out from the hospital.

I was on the flight line working when the explosion happened and we initially thought that the building that held the AIM-7 missiles blew up and so we took immediate cover as the AIM-7 warheads held some nasty expanding steel bands for destroying aircraft in flight! Later that day, after that area was cleared by Explosive Ordinance Disposal (EOD) personnel, some of us went over there and could see that not all the body parts had been cleaned up! That was quite traumatic to see what was left of someone I knew. A "brain fart" at the wrong time in our line of work often caused injuries or death.

In fact a "brain fart" by another load crew resulted in a bad injury to Steve Wojnar one night while we were performing a functional check on one of our F-4s. This other crew had "safed" the jet by removing the ejector cartridges prior to us uploading it for its next mission. Trouble was that they failed to remove the carts from the center line ejector rack, but then signed it off as being safe for the upload.

One of my tasks as the number two man on our crew was to sit in the cockpit and activate various switches during the functional check, while Steve checked for firing voltage with a PSM-6 multimeter. We always started at the left outboard pylon and bomb rack, then the inboard pylon, and then the centerline rack followed by the right pylons. The accident happened when we got to the centerline rack. The two ejector cartridges had not been removed so Steve started to unscrew the caps that contained the firing pins and our crew chief SSgt Jim Riley assumed that he was checking for firing voltage and gave me the hand signal to push the jettison switch!

As soon as I did that I heard a loud "blap" and looked down to see Steve rolling on the ground from under the jet and screaming with smoke coming from his hand! He had got the first cap loose and removed the cartridge and had started to unscrew the second one when I pushed the switch to send 28 volts to the rack! The gas pellets in the second cart then immediately ignited and blew into the breach that Steve had just opened and the force blew them into his hand while they were still burning.

He was out of commission for a week or so after that and the incident was labeled a "stray voltage accident" since neither my crew chief nor I fessed up to the real cause! There were two "brain farts" that caused it. First was the crew who failed to remove the carts. Second, Steve saw that the carts hadn't been removed and should have stopped the functional check. Even Steve thought that it was stray voltage that caused the cart to blow and I kept him into the dark about what really happened until right before we left Thailand. He was really pissed off then but then got over it. Luckily it was only his hand and not his eyes.

One morning I had got back to my hootch after a night of work and was sound asleep when all of a sudden there was a loud explosion and at the same time me and my bunk rose up in the air and crashed back down to the floor with stuff rattling off the metal roof! What happened was one of our jets returning from a combat mission had a "one lugger", which was a bomb that didn't fully release when dropped and was still attached to the bomb rack by one of the two lugs.

When the jet made a sharp turn into the landing pattern it let go and being armed, exploded on impact about 500 yards from my hootch in a rice paddy or field. Luckily no one was hurt. So after being reassured that we weren't under attack it was back to sleep.

One morning I was woke up by shots being fired close to my hootch and that was the Thai security police on base driving around and shooting the stray dogs that were running loose on the base. They would get them cornered, shoot them with shotguns and just leave them lay so we would have to endure the stench until they rotted away. Most of these dogs were completely hairless from mange or other maladies and were not nice to look at. They ran around in packs on the base and we were told to never touch them.

One incident that has stuck with me emotionally ever since it happened on the flight line had to do with a returning jet from a combat mission. We were waiting for it to park and shut down so we could remove the bomb racks and any unexpended ordnance. It had been carrying four LAU-3A rocket pods that held 19 2.75 inch rockets each which were now empty signifying a successful mission or so we believed.

When the pilot, a major, got down from the cockpit he was all smiles and proceeded to tell us that he had saved us some work by expending the high explosive rockets on a couple of villagers sitting by a cooking fire by a rice paddy. What? He was so bombastic in his words and attitude that we hoped he was just bullshitting us but the more he went on about it we knew he was serious. So two innocent people had to die to save us some work. How noble of that fucking asshole killer major. What a warrior he was to make war on non-combatants. No wonder our countries' reputation sucked over there when jerks like that are let loose. I guess "war is hell" in many ways.

Due to the nature of my profession I understood that I was complicit also in wartime death and destruction of enemy combatants on a daily basis. So in that regard I guess I had to also be considered an accomplice to murder due to this pilot's action.

We talked about it and came to terms with it individually, or so I remember but saying anything about it would have gone nowhere in a military environment. I was still a teenager in thoughts, words and deeds. I was certainly confused and troubled by the whole incident.

The "Killer Major" was the exception though because when we met the jets returning from their missions we enjoyed hearing the harrowing details and stories from the pilots. I had read details from a book by William Manchester about his experiences during World War II. In it he said, "Much of the evil in the world has been done in the name of honor." I guess the major believed that what he did was honorable but I saw it as anything but.

One of the strangest events a friend and I happened upon one day in the town of Ubon. It was at an open where some guys were herding pigs up on the bed of a truck. When they filled it up, all of sudden we heard the pigs squealing like mad because the guys were cutting the pig's throats. There were torrents of blood running to the ground. When there was no more squealing or movement they laid a bamboo mat over the dead pigs and herded another layer of pigs on top of them.

Then the second layer was dispatched in the same way. Then the same with a third layer. Now the truck was full of dead bleeding out pigs and off they went with the blood dripping all over the road. I guess they had never heard of blood sausage.

One early evening after a twelve hour shift Bob Dumey, Steve Wojnar and I were in the Airmen's Club at a table having some drinks when a small group of guys we had never seen before came in and were very loud and going around the main club room and asking something at several tables. One table of guys started pointing at us and we thought "oh shit," why are they looking for us because we had never seen them before? So here they come to our table and asked us if we were in the 25th TFS. We said, "Yes we are and what of it?" Well, they immediately started patting us on the back and shaking our hands and informed us that we were going to the bars in Ubon and everything was on them!

Why? Because they were in a Marine combat unit in Vietnam and came to Ubon on their R&R (rest and recreation) to look up the Air Force F-4 fighters that saved their butts during a firefight while surrounded by an NVA (North Vietnamese Army) unit. Our jets had come in so low to releasing weapons on the NVA that the Marines could see the tail letters identifying the squadron. That was FP on our jets. They did some investigating and found out that it was our squadron jets.

Loading a 750 pound bomb at Ubon

Since they were enlisted and our pilots were officers they couldn't party with them so we were the next best thing. They were really thrilled to know that we had loaded the weapons on the jets. We partied with them for two nights downtown as at that point we were three days on and two days off. We were all wined and dined for two days courtesy of those crazy Marines. Since they had a weeklong R&R they later partied with some other weapons guys from our shop during their days off. Of course everything paid for by them.

Dave Moe at Ubon, Thailand

One morning, while walking to work, I met Dave Moe, a Milan High School classmate! At first we both said a casual hello to each other as we passed. It sunk in a split second later that we knew each other in another life! What a shock that was! He had just arrived there as an F-4 crew chief in the 435th TFS. We hung out a lot together on and off base after that and it was so good to catch up on or share the local news from back home when we received mail. I would see him on the flight line at work quite a lot and one time helped him to launch his jet by pulling wheel chocks at his signal!

Since we were reassigned from the 25th TFS to the 8th TFW we were under the control of the Headquarters Squadron and therefore subjected to fill their extra duty slots, one of which was as an Air Police augmentee to perform base security. Bob Dumey, Steve Wojnar and I had to attend a classes on weapons handling and maintenance and then go to the firing range where we were allowed to fire the M-16 on full auto and also to fire the 7.62 caliber M-60 machine gun. How cool was that? The firing range was out in the Thai countryside. While we were doing all our shooting requirements, a large number of Thai kids would scamper among us and scavenge up all the empty brass cartridges our weapons were ejecting. The Air Police in charge of the training tried to keep them away but to no avail! The brass casings translated to income for those kids and their families.

After the training was completed we were on call for base perimeter security detail where we would be assigned a guard post for an eight hour shift. The worst part of this was that we had to wear a helmet and a heavy flak jacket for the duration. After only an hour or so the weight of that flak jacket was so painful that it was almost unbearable.

We also carried a 2-way radio and were instructed to call into the Central Security Control if we were fired upon, and to ask permission before we could return fire! Yeah right! If someone was trying to kill me I was going to shoot back and to hell with an OK from someone sitting at a desk in safety. I defer to the popular saying "I'd rather be judged by twelve than be carried by six"! Finally our commitment as security augmenters was completed and then back to our main duties.

The flight line at Ubon. There were 96 F-4s in the 8ᵗʰ TFW there.

My year in Thailand was finally up in June of 1969 and after numerous "short" parties and a farewell to Dave Moe, I boarded a C-130 Hercules cargo plane to Bangkok to spend a night prior to the "freedom bird" flight the next day to home and the "land of the big BX"!

When our flight left from Ubon, it was without Steve Wojnar whom had contracted hepatitis and was in the hospital under quarantine! What happened was that about a week before we were all to leave I had noticed that Steve's eyes were getting real yellow and since I had experience with that as a teenager I told him that he should get a doctor's checkup. He got worried about it, had the checkup and was then immediately confined to a hospital bed.

Since I had already had hepatitis I got to go and visit him and was he ever pissed off at me! Especially since they told him he couldn't leave with us but had to be medically evacuated to a hospital in the States. Even 45 years later he still reminds me of that!

As soon as we got to Bangkok and assigned rooms to sleep in, it was a quick change into civvies and off to the Bangkok bars for one last Thailand party! I only remember getting back to where we were staying after daylight and sleeping through the day until our flight out that evening on the "freedom bird" to Travis AFB outside of San Francisco, California.

After landing and getting off the plane, there literally were some guys getting on their knees and kissing the ground being so happy to be home, only to arise to the jeering, taunts, and name calling from the constant, daily, anti-war crowd on the other side of a chain link fence by the terminal. It was one thing to experience that with school kids in Denver but here these assholes were mature adults! There was no response from any of us either because we were kind of in shock seeing fellow American people behave that way.

It was just as bad during the bus ride through San Francisco to the airport on a blue Air Force bus. There were even professionals wearing business suits on the sidewalks who would holler some expletive while giving us the "finger"! But after getting to the airport and while still in uniform at a bar to get something to drink, I never had to pay for anything. Several travelers insisted on honoring my service by paying for anything I wanted! Go figure. Lots of mixed signals there! I guess running the "gauntlet" of the assholes in San Francisco was my version of Post-Traumatic Stress Disorder (PTSD). I made myself a promise to never visit that city again during my lifetime.

My new orders was an assignment to the 57th Fighter Weapons Squadron at Nellis AFB in Las Vegas, Nevada and I was really looking forward to going there.

My brother Lynn and his now wife Carol Winkleman picked me up from the Minneapolis airport and back to Montevideo where my parents now lived at 115 North 9th Street, having moving off the farm while I was in Thailand. Dad took a job with the city as the sexton at the Sunset Cemetery, since it was easier work and paid better than as a cash rent farmer. I really missed the farm but it wasn't my calling.

It was so good to be with the family again and of course Mom and Dad wanted to show me off and insisted that I go to church with them in uniform! I insisted, "No way," after my experience in San Francisco. They weren't happy about that but finally accepted my decision. I just didn't want to be a visible target for another asshole!

Getting my own car was a priority and I test drove and bought, or I should say the bank bought, a new 1968 Dodge Charger which was metallic gold in color and had a 383 cubic inch engine that put out 330 horsepower. As soon as the loan paperwork was signed and I picked it up, I immediately drove it down to Brandon Tire shop and had new *American Magnesium* wheels put on it. That really made it a head turner!

After spending time with the family and seeing relatives and friends again it was off to my next assignment at Nellis AFB, Nevada. Since I hadn't saved much money during my year in Thailand, having spent most of it on partying and such, Grandpa Weckhorst gave me gas money for the two day drive. I was really happy for that. I spent the first night in Denver, Colorado and then made it to Las Vegas the next night. Back then there was no speed limit on the interstate highway in Nevada so was pretty cool to cruise at 120 MPH for a number of miles. Dangerous yes, but my car had a 150 MPH speedometer so 120 MPH was nothing! I was a 21 year old "kid" so I was invincible!

After finding the base and signing in at the billeting office, I got a room for a couple days at a "black" casino in North Las Vegas. It was under contract to the base and then another life chapter started.

Chapter 22

Nellis AFB, Nevada

Ready for a military parade at Nellis AFB 1969

My fellow crew member Bob Dumey was also assigned to Nellis but his orders were to the new F-111 Wing and mine were to the 57th Fighter Weapons Squadron and back on F-4s. After Thailand I wanted, more than anything, to be done with the F-4 and tried to pull a fast one. I made an attempt to process into the F-111 Wing with Bob. I actually made it through several of the in-processing requirements until a real observant clerk read my orders and figured out what I was attempting to do!

I didn't get into trouble for it but was told in no uncertain terms that I was in violation of official regulations and to go where I was ordered! Oh well, I tried! Later on though I was glad that I didn't get to the F-111s because Bob Dumey was just miserable there with all the bullshit and chickenshit details that a new unit had to go through.

Since my squadron was a training unit, we really had it good compared to Eglin AFB and Ubon. We were busy only during certain intervals of the pilot's training schedule. After a year in a wartime environment made up of real combat operations, it was very hard to transition to the "stateside" way of doing our job and the mundane "by the book" requirements that we deemed not necessary in real wartime operations.

I loved Las Vegas. For a 21 year old it was a dream assignment with the casinos, headliner shows and the night life that translated into around the clock fun! I was never a gambler and only did that as a means to an end. A 2 dollar roll of nickels at a slot machine and played slowly and strategically meant a constant flow of free cocktails and a real good "buzz" before hitting the nightclubs where the drinks weren't free!

In 1969 Las Vegas had a population of around 250 to 300 thousand people, and now (2013) the population is around 2 million, so back then it was still a fairly small city.

There was a dress code in casinos back then and blue jeans were not allowed. A coat and tie was even required for some of the headliner shows. Nowadays, anything goes, no matter the condition or appearance. What happened to pride in one's appearance!

Las Vegas was also known for inexpensive food and with breakfasts costing only 49 cents that was quite the draw. When I worked the midnight to 7 A.M. shift, and after our initial training weapons uploads were complete, we changed into civilian clothes and instead of going the chow hall we headed to downtown Las Vegas to the *El Cortez Casino* for breakfast. The breakfasts were better down there this also afforded us the opportunity to throw a few coins in a slot machine!

One day I was walking somewhere on base when up walked Steve Moser! I first met him at Eglin AFB in Florida and he was from Nevada, Iowa. He was a farm boy like me and we had become friends while we were stationed down there. After the shock of seeing each other again, we quickly renewed our friendship and hung out together most of the time.

Other than cruising the casinos and partying away the weekends, the one thing we really enjoyed together was attending and occasionally participating in the drag racing at the Las Vegas race track. Moe (Steve Moser) had bought a new Dodge Super Bee with a higher horsepower motor than mine. He entered it in the bracket races and we took turns racing it against other cars.

I was so proud of and enamored with my 68 Dodge Charger that instead of hunting for parking spots in the casino lots, I utilized valet parking where I drove up to the front entrance doors and handed the keys to an attendant and for a couple bucks he parked it for me! The Charger was metallic gold with new magnesium wheels and it was a real head turner. I would really get a "big head" hearing the admiring comments of people who were going into the casino. They would be staring at it before it was driven off!

Eventually I sold the Charger as it was becoming a financial burden. The monthly loan payment and insurance took up about half of my pay and since it was also a real gas guzzler, the need for cheaper transportation had arrived.

1968 Charger bought new. Nellis Air Force Base. Very valuable now to collectors. Fifty grand?

At Lake Mead, Nevada outside of Las Vegas. 1970

I then purchased a used Opal Kadett which was way smaller, and with a four cylinder motor it was much cheaper to drive. It wasn't nearly as cool as the Charger but it worked.

One night, while bar hopping with another friend, I was sitting at a major intersection waiting for the traffic light to change when all of a sudden my car was surrounded by police squad cars with lights flashing and officers rushing towards us with guns drawn and shouting at us to keep our hands where they could see them! We were told to get out of the car where they spread-eagled us and searched us. This was being done all the while with numerous guns pointed at us. W.T.F.! We kept asking, what did we do? What did we do? But no response from them yet.

We were then handcuffed and put in the back of a squad car and driven off. Finally one of the police officers told us that they were taking us out to Henderson to be identified by the owner of a motel that was robbed at gunpoint by two men driving a small yellow car. Since my Opal Kadett was small and yellow, we were prime suspects.

We soon arrived at the motel and the owner came out to the car, looked in at us and said that we weren't the robbers. That was very good news. I was expecting to be brought back to my car and released, but no, the night didn't end there! We were then taken to the Clark

County Jail where we were booked on suspicion of armed robbery and possession of cheating devices, the "devices" being a small bag of slot machine tokens from the *Mint Casino*! This was apparently done for the purpose of keeping us off the streets as they knew we had been drinking and to punish us because of our constant smart-ass comments on their treatment of us. Alcohol induced, of course!

We were then taken to a cell and strip searched and put in another holding cell with a number of other "prisoners" like us. We spent the night in the jail until we were released the next morning to an officer from the squadron. All the charges were dropped!

Around that time, my then girlfriend had given me a stick-on American flag, to put on the rear window of my car. It was in the shape of a "peace" symbol. I thought it was pretty cool but apparently someone else didn't and reported it to the base commander. One day at work I got a call from the orderly room to report to the base commander at a certain time. I had no idea what it was about. After reporting to him for a lecture on patriotism and how wrong it was to display the flag that way, I was ordered to remove it immediately. This was witnessed by someone from his office and the issue was dropped! By then my discharge date couldn't arrive soon enough!

On December 5th of 1970, the day had finally arrived and since Steve Moser was also discharged the same time and going back to Iowa for a short time, we rented a tow bar and towed my Opel behind his Super Bee to Omaha, Nebraska. We parted with the understanding that in a month or two we would reunite for a return trip to Las Vegas as civilians and to get jobs in a casino.

Chapter 23

Home Again

It was great to be back home again even though it wasn't the farm. Dad had since gave up farming and took a job in Montevideo as the Sexton, or caretaker, of the large Sunset Cemetery on the north side of town. And so they bought a house at 115 North 9th Street and now lived there. I liked it though because Monte was at least the center of what social life there was and so it was right out the front door.

I had every intention of going back to Las Vegas with Steve Moser to find work and to return to a girlfriend that I met there a couple months earlier and really liked but it was not to be. One night in Torgerson's clothing store downtown I ran into my high school sweetheart whom I had dated for several years but that had ended when I got the "Dear John" letter from her while I was in Thailand. Well, we hit it off again and started seeing each other on her weekend's home from college and that influenced me to call Steve to tell him I was staying home! In the end though I should have went with him as my girlfriend and I couldn't overcome our differences and grew apart again.

Dad's cousin Clifford Skogrand was the manager at the Farmers Union Co-op down behind Main Street and offered me a job there as a shop mechanic and so I took it at a whopping $1.10 an hour! It was spending money though and since I was living with Mom and Dad and eating their food I had enough for my needs. And I liked working on cars also!

Arnie Thompson was one of the District State Highway Patrol Officers and would occasionally bring his squad car in for servicing at the Co-op. I got to know him fairly well and one day he asked me if I would be interested in doing what he did! I said "sure" and so he arranged for me to apply for entrance into the Highway Patrol Academy. I was scheduled to take the entrance exams in several months, but before the date I received a letter from the Highway Patrol Office stating that since there were eight graduates from the previous class that still hadn't been placed, that the 1971 class would be cancelled until further notice!

I sure had hopes for that but it was not to be. Montevideo was quickly becoming a "dead end" for me. Anyone I used to hang out with before I went in the Air Force had either moved away or were married so I needed a change. I had considered going back out to Las Vegas again but Steve Moser had since got married out there and was moving back to Iowa to take over his dad's farm. I had also applied and was accepted at Southwest State College in Marshall but I really had no interest in that at the time either.

In the meantime I met Debbie George at her cousin's wedding dance out at the M&M Ballroom between Montevideo and Watson and though I didn't realize it at the time she was to become my wife a year later. She was from Litchfield and it wasn't long before I spent every weekend driving back and forth from home to there. I worked at the Co-op for about a year and then quit to take a better paying job at Chandler Industries with my brother Lynn. This was a machinist company that manufactured various metal parts and pieces and I soon realized that standing at a machine for 10 hours a day was not for me.

Then I took a job at the Co-op fertilizer plant working for Mike Jorgenson applying anhydrous ammonia on fields in the area but soon realized that sitting on a tractor all day didn't appeal to me either so I quit that and took a job with my brother Ron building ceilings for mobile homes at Regal Homes down in Smiths Addition.

One day when I was working at the Co-op a couple young guys from Minneapolis pulled up outside in a huge 1960 Cadillac limousine, came in the shop and asked me if I knew anyone interested in buying their car! It was really cool looking and I asked, "How much? They said $250, as they needed money bad. They had the title so I bought it on the spot! One of them had bought it from a funeral home where it was used to drive the grieving family during a funeral. This car held nine people, with an electric sliding window separating the front seat from the rear, two separate air conditioners and two radio systems!

I quickly put wide whitewall porto-walls on the tires to make it more period looking and sure had a good time driving it around town. Dad liked driving it too and one day he drove it downtown for something. Since Monte had angled parking, it was way too long for that. I drove up Main Street on my way home from work and there was my limo sticking way out in the street with Dad nowhere in sight! He never thought it would block traffic like it did.

My 1960 Cadillac Limo purchased for $ 250.00

The little yellow Opel Kadett that I brought back from Las Vegas finally met its end one morning! I was sleeping in late one morning and was woken up by a loud crashing noise outside. Pretty soon Dad came upstairs and told me that someone had ran into the rear of my car and had "accordioned" it between his van and my limousine! Since the limo was twice as big and heavy as the Opel, the damage was severe enough to "total" out the car with the insurance company. Since the limo was too much of a gas hog to drive daily I needed other wheels and quickly resolved that issue.

Terry Fonkert lived in Hector, MN at the time and called me one day to tell me about a 1970 AAR Plymouth Barracuda "Cuda" that was sitting in Whitte Ford in downtown Hector. He told me to get down there fast to look at it before it was sold, so off I went. As soon as I walked in and saw it I knew it was mine, and after a quick test drive to burn some rubber off the tires we did the deal. It was an electric blue color with a black interior, a 340 cubic inch engine with a "6 pack" carburetor setup (3 2-barrel carburetors) and rated at a light 290 horsepower, controlled by a 4-speed transmission with a pistol grip shifter. I was in heaven!

My 1970 AAR "Cuda." A rare model I should have
kept. It may sell for $125,000 now.

This was absolutely the coolest car around and was I ever proud of it. The loan officer at Northwest Bank in Monte wasn't happy about it though because I had to have pre-authorization back then to buy a car and was only allowed to borrow $1,800 because of my income. Well, the Cuda was $2300 and when I went to tell him what I bought, he was pissed! But the damage was done and after a good ass-chewing the loan was completed.

At least I lucked out with cheap insurance though because even though the Cuda would beat anything on the road in a drag race, it was only rated at 290 horsepower which was under the 300 HP that determined the higher rates for high performance engines. It was a true "muscle car" of the muscle car era and is now a very highly sought after collector car routinely selling for a hundred thousand dollars or more in "like new" condition!

Occasionally I would take the Cuda down to Minnesota Dragways in Coon Rapids to enter it in the races there. My one claim to fame there was racing it against Alan Page of the Minnesota Vikings and his 1970

Plymouth GTX that was painted purple and had large gold letters on the side reading "Purple people eater", named after the Vikings defensive front four. Needless to say I lost to him and his dealer maintained car! It sure was pretty though.

I kept the Cuda for a little over a year but it had started to burn a little oil so I sold it for a pretty good price to Eric Jorgenson of Montevideo. The last I heard of it was that he resold it and it was currently a "show" car out in Las Vegas, whatever that meant.

I next bought a dark green 1969 Dodge Charger and drove that for a couple years more. In the meantime Deb and I were married on August 5th of 1972 at Zion Methodist Church in Litchfield by Pastor Larry Foote. After a honeymoon to the north shore of Lake Superior, we settled into an upstairs apartment in Montevideo where I was still working on trailer houses.

Our wedding August 5th, 1972 at Zion Methodist
Church in Litchfield, Minnesota

The local Air Force recruiter at the time was Larry Peart who was a family friend of Deb's parents. I got to know him fairly well and he would occasionally give me surplus .30-06 caliber ammunition that he couldn't use. One day he asked me if I had ever given thought to going back in the Air Force. My response was "hell no" until he informed me that the pay had almost doubled since I got out and that if I went back in before a two year deadline that I could also keep my old rank of Sergeant. I then asked him what, exactly, would my monthly pay be and he told me that it was twice what I was currently making then. I really started thinking about it and comparing it to my current occupation and what the future would be by staying in Montevideo.

The outlook didn't look so good so I started talking to Deb about it and how she felt about an Air Force life. I guess the determining factor for me was that I could choose where I wanted to be stationed so I thought, why not? I informed the recruiter and was then scheduled for another physical. I had to go through the same routine as before and wouldn't you know it, the same huge black guy that stabbed my finger for blood back in 1966 was still there doing the same job. Again, my finger ached for a week after he stabbed it with what felt like a butcher knife!

I passed the physical again so then came the choice of where I wanted to be stationed if I re-enlisted. I wanted nothing to do with the F-4 again and since the A-7 Corsair was fairly new to the Air Force and was stationed at Davis-Monthan AFB in Tucson, Arizona, that's where I wanted to go. Well, the Air Force said OK! And so I signed back up and soon had orders to report there in November of 1972.

Before reenlisting in 1972. Dad was getting ready to cut my hair.

Deb and I prior to my leaving for Utapao, Thailand for a year 1974

Our parents weren't real happy about us moving across the country but understood that it was good for us and so after numerous Minnesota goodbyes and packing up all our belongings in the car, we were off to a new life!

On the way to Arizona we stopped off in Emporia, Kansas and spent a couple days with Deb's brother Steve and his family of Marion and Brent and Bach, their huge St. Bernard dog.

After we left them and got closer to the rest of our life, I was getting more and more stressed about what to expect when I got there and how much the Air Force had changed in the last two years. At the same time I was eager to get back into a profession that I considered myself very good at. I was soon to find out that my previous skills hadn't diminished at all. This was my calling in life.

Chapter 24

Back to the Air Force

Davis-Monthan AFB, Arizona

My load crew in Hawaii, John Horton, Mike Palmer and Jim Jenkins

An A-7

In front of one of our A-7s in Hawaii

Tucson was a large city with Davis-Monthan AFB taking up a huge area on the south side of it. After signing in on base and getting my in-processing schedule we went apartment hunting and found one we liked at 6171 E. Bellevue Ave, Apt 12, about a block off Speedway Ave which was a main "artery" road in Tucson.

I had kept some of my old uniforms from my first enlistment but the fatigues weren't in very good shape so the first order of business was to get new ones with my clothing allowance. In-processing took about a week and then on to load crew training as a crew chief in the 355th Munitions Maintenance Squadron Weapons Loading Section.

The A-7 was pretty new to the Air Force and was used mainly as a close air support attack fighter. Compared to the F-4 it was almost a joy to work on as it was less labor intensive. The main reason why I really didn't enjoy my time there was because I was put on "mid" shift, which was from midnight to 7:00 A.M. I was on this shift for most of my time there and so was the reason I volunteered to go anyplace else.

Since I worked at night and slept most of the day, and it being Arizona, was hot as hell during the day, I had a hard time being out in the hot sun on weekends and it put limits on what I did on my off time. And on weekends Deb was used to going to bed at a normal time and I was used to being up all night so it was awkward for us in that regard.

Other than that though, we did enjoy our time there. We would occasionally go camping up on Mount Lemon, or make occasional trips down to Nogales, Mexico, or just generally enjoy the area around Tucson and the city itself.

One of the most detested people I had ever known in my Air Force career was a Chief Master Sergeant Cain who was the maintenance superintendent of our squadron. His supervision was based mainly on intimidation and humiliation of subordinates. An example of this was that for any infraction of our duties, any minor mistake, was grounds for a briefing at each shift change by the offender as to why it happened and why it wouldn't happen again!

I had to do it once over a paperwork mistake which meant I had to brief the day shift and come in at 4:00 P.M. to brief the swing shift, and then my own shift at midnight. I had heard through the grapevine, that the younger airmen on mid shifts that were detailed to make his coffee for when he came in to work, would pee in the water in the coffee pot in retaliation of his just being a jerk, but I never witnessed it, but nor would I drink any coffee!

My most memorable time there was when my crew and I were chosen to accompany 6 A-7s to Kaneohe Marine Corps Air Station in Hawaii for a 3 month deployment in support of the Army 25th Infantry Division flying close air support. It was basically 3 months on the beach as we only worked about a half day shift throughout the deployment. One of the nicest beaches on the island was on the Marine base and was where most of our off time was spent and where I got pretty good at body surfing.

Chapter 25

Utapao Royal Thai Air Base, Thailand

My desire to leave Davis-Monthan AFB resulted in orders to report to Utapao RTAFB situated on the Gulf of Siam. Not that I wanted to go back to Thailand but I was looking forward to a change.

After a 30 day leave back home, it was a teary goodbye to Deb at the Minneapolis Airport and off I went to Travis AFB, California for the military charter flight to Thailand for twelve months.

Once processing was complete and in my seat, I met my seatmate Duane Shaeffer whom I was to work with for the next year! Our first stop on the flight was Anchorage, Alaska where we deplaned for several hours for refueling. Once back on board I took my shoes off and was ready for some serious sleep on the next leg of the flight to Yokota, Japan. While the plane taxied to the runway Duane said that I should keep my shoes on till we were in the air because "you never know"! A premonition? So I re-laced my shoes and upon takeoff roll the airplane started shaking violently and wouldn't quit.

Of course there was major panic and finally the plane slowed to a stop at the far end of the runway. Then everything was calm until I spotted flames through the wing flaps below where I was seated. A stewardess was walking by assuring us that everything was fine until I told her there was a fire under the wing! She immediately ran to the front of the plane and then the warning to "Evacuate, evacuate, evacuate" came over the speakers. Then real panic set in. The emergency exits were opened and the slides inflated and out I jumped when it was my turn. I hit the ground running and it was "assholes and elbows" for several hundred yards! Sure glad I put my shoes back on. The whole underside of the plane was, by then, in flames but was quickly put out by the airport firemen.

We couldn't get back on the plane to get any personal belongings yet so we were bused to the main terminal and told that drinks were "on the house" in the bars while we waited. After several hours of "stress relief" we were finally allowed back on the plane to get our stuff and then were taken in to Anchorage and put up in motels.

The next day we were re-boarded on the same plane, as the landing gear had been replaced and nothing else was damaged, and took off for Japan! I had everything crossed that I could on that takeoff!

The cause of the incident was blown landing gear wheels from running over some jagged metal and of the 300 or so of us, about 30 people had broken legs and arms from jumping off the wings. And to this day, I hate flying.

After an uneventful stopover in Japan it was on to Thailand and after in-processing and barracks assignment it was off to my new work area and to meet my supervisors. I was assigned to the Loading Standardization Crew which was in charge of all weapons load training of the B-52D bomber. My new boss, SMSgt Fitch assigned me as the crew chief but I adamantly refused as I had zero experience on the B-52 and so was made a team member.

I just couldn't see myself running a training program on a system I wasn't trained on myself, and had no experience on. I played centerfield or rover on our squadron fast pitch softball team during that season and even played some basketball for the squadron but mostly warmed the bench! Other off duty time was spent mostly at the library or going to a movie at one of the two movie theatres, one being an outdoor theatre out at the beach where the movie was sometimes drowned out by B-52s taking off or landing.

We had a wing of about eighteen B-52s on the flight line.

On the flight line ready to up load weapons on a B-52

After about six months there, I had Deb fly over to stay for as long as allowed and I found a two story bungalow down in Banchang which was a small village about five miles from the base. We settled in nice there but it took her several sleepless nights to get used to the lizards on the walls and ceilings and the huge cockroaches. The first night there, a lizard actually fell on the bed while we were in it. She shed a few tears over that, ha! Eventually she grew accustomed to life there and kind of enjoyed it, I think!

We had to go to Bangkok every couple of weeks to renew her passport and while there stayed at the Florida Hotel somewhere near the central part of that huge city. Our first taxi driver that drove us around the city was Chai Vichai and we became good friends and so we were in his charge whenever we went there. He was a constant companion and even invited us to his home to meet his family. That was a very humble experience as his whole home was about the size of a standard American bedroom. We had a hard time trying to understand how he, his wife and small children could live in such a small place. But, it was enough for them and they were happy and they would probably think that it was odd for us to live like we do here!

Chai Vichai, Deb and me in Bangkok

Deb and I did some cooking down at our bungalow but usually would take a small taxi out to the base and eat supper in the USO club. It was a welcome break for her after being cooped up in the bungalow all day while I was at work. She liked going to the movies on base and even the outdoor theatre, even though some nights the only pop they had was Dr. Pepper and maybe some stale popcorn! After about 2 ½ months Deb finally flew back home as she would have had to leave the country to get her passport renewed, and since that meant crossing the border into Cambodia we decided the risk wasn't worth it because of previous problems there. So off she went and I was back in the barracks.

Our barracks was divided up into cubicles with 4 people each. I lucked out with some pretty good roommates though one evening as I was writing a letter home or something, one of my roommates came running into the room saying "the cops are coming", and proceeded to grab a box out of his locker and run back out the door! Here the Air Police come with drug sniffing dogs to go through each room. What my roommate was doing was buying Thai stick, which was marijuana laced with heroin and packaging it up and sending it back to friends back in the states. The dogs didn't alert on our room that night but my roommate and I and the other two had a brief discussion about that not happening again! I would have been guilty by association had he been caught!

It was pure drudgery living in the barracks again after Deb left. We were always off doing something together when not at work and the time really flew by. Now with her gone the rest of my year there slowed to a snail's crawl and orders for my next assignment couldn't come soon enough.

I was hoping to get Mountain Home AFB in Idaho as my next base since it was my first choice, and, sure enough, I got my orders for there finally. Now I spent my free time getting as much information as I could about Idaho in the library and was really excited about all the great hunting and fishing opportunities there.

As before, and just like returning to the U.S. from Ubon Thailand, we had to run the gauntlet of protesters and name callers in San Francisco. And that is why I will never, ever, set foot in that city again.

Chapter 26

Mountain Home AFB, Idaho

After a short leave back home it was off to Idaho and our next adventure. The drive there was great with some gorgeous scenery in Wyoming. We stayed overnight in Jackson Hole and then on to Mountain Home the next day. It was getting more barren the closer we got to the town of Mountain Home but then the drive out to the base which was about 8 miles south of the town was even worse.

Deb actually was tearing up a little wondering what we were getting ourselves into as there were tumbleweeds rolling across the road and even I was getting somewhat skeptical about our new home! The real mountains that I assumed that Mt. Home was surrounded by were miles away to the north!

After checking into base billeting where we spent several nights, we were assigned quarters on base at 4323B Mountain Village. It was an apartment building with 4 residences with 2 stories each. We became fast friends with the other tenants and did lots of activities together.

The F-111 F model was the fighter/bomber assigned to the 366th TFW, and I was to be a weapons load team chief in the 366th MMS loading section. I was told, when I first reported to my new boss, that I was to be given the worst load crew in the section but that I should be able to handle them since I was a Staff Sergeant! Was he ever right. They were Ron Rairdon, Dan Ragan, and Randy Saeger. Names I will never forget! They were very good at their jobs but had a terrible attitude problem with authority so it was a constant headache keeping them in line.

I fell into the mistake of becoming too friendly with them too and they soon found ways to take advantage of me when they could, until I eventually came to understand the difference between friendship and leadership. So after I finally gained real respect from them all was good and we became one of the top load crews.

The hunting and fishing opportunities were the main reasons that I wanted to be stationed in Idaho. I soon became fast friends with Wayne Jernigan, a fellow crew chief, and we were always together hunting ducks and geese during the season. We hunted ducks mainly on the Bruneau River south of the base or on a lake northeast of Mountain Home, about 30 miles away. We also went elk hunting north of Boise but never saw any.

My other passion was softball and I played the "rover" position on our squadron team. In one game I "hit for the cycle", which was a single, a double, a triple and a home run and so made the base paper because of it. We were a very good team but were only second best of all the squadron teams by getting beat in the season ending championship game against the Avionics squadron.

On my way to a squadron softball game.

Our firstborn son Jesse was born to us in the base hospital on the 10th of March 1976, and in preparation for his birth we had enrolled in Lamaze classes that stressed breathing control during the labor and birth process instead of drug inducement.

We went to classes at the hospital for several months and I thought I had the "coaching" requirements down pat but on the night of the labor and birth I pretty much forgot all I learned due to the excitement I was feeling and finally was instructed by the doctor to stand back by the wall so that the birth would take place under their methods. All went well and we were blessed with our new son. We had no idea if we would have a boy or girl and so had names picked either way.

In the meantime, I had received orders for Bitburg Air Base in Germany so when Jesse was 4 months old we left Mountain Home for a 30 day leave in Minnesota with our families and then on to our next adventure in Germany.

Chapter 27

Bitburg Air Base, Germany

At Bitburg, AFB

After an uneventful flight to Rhein-Main Air Base in Frankfurt, except for jet lag, we took a bus to Bitburg Air Base where we stayed in billeting until we found an apartment downtown. We rented this apartment for about 3 or 4 months until we were finally assigned housing on base. There were 8 apartments in the stairwell and we were in 41E3 which was Apt E on the 3rd floor of building 41.

We became good friends with most everyone in the stairwell, and very close friends with Pete and Renate Bailey and their children Sandra and Michael. They became very attached to Jesse and so we spent a lot of time together.

I was assigned to the 36th Munitions Maintenance Squadron as a crew chief again on the F-4! As much as I liked that jet I hated to work on it but it wouldn't be for long as the fighter wing was soon to transition to the new F-15 Air Superiority Fighter which would only carry AIM-7 and AIM-9 missiles and an internal 20mm Gatling gun.

As for off time and entertainment we traveled a lot throughout Germany and to the countries of Luxembourg, Belgium, Austria and Switzerland as they were so close to us. Luxembourg was only about 15 miles away. During WW II Patton's 3rd Army had destroyed a number of huge bunkers not far from Bitburg.

My parents came to visit us after we had been there about a year and so we traveled to the Black Forest and down to Garmisch where we stayed at an armed forces recreation hotel for several days. They really loved Germany.

My brother Lynn and his wife Carol also came over the following summer and we also travelled for a week in southern Germany and into Switzerland and Austria. Had a great time with them and saw a lot of great sights.

Deb's parents Don and Shirley also came over for a week not long after Lynn & Carol left for home and since I had already taken leave time with Lynn & Carol, I had a difficult time getting any more time off that soon but did manage to get several more days and so we went down to Munich and stayed there for 3 or 4 days. We also had a great time with them.

One rather hilarious event happened while we were staying down in Garmisch with Lynn and Carol. One day we decided to take a cable car up to the summit of the Wankbahn, which was a mountain nearest the city. There were probably about 30 of us in the car, us being the only non-German. About halfway up someone, not us, let go an unbelievably stinky SBD (silent but deadly) fart. It stunk so bad and since all these Germans were all stone-faced about it, Lynn and I started giggling. And we couldn't stop and the other riders were giving us the evil eye, including the real guilty one. We literally could not stop once we got the "giggles" and could not wait for the ride to end. Deb and Carol were more embarrassed than we were. It sure was funny though.

Football was the big competitive sport with all the air bases in Europe and on game day the whole military community attended. It was very high caliber competition on about an NCAA Division 2 level with mostly college level players. Bitburg was the perennial Germany champion and would end up playing the top team from the U.K. (United Kingdom) and won the championship the 3 years we were there. And we never missed a home game!

In the spring of 1977 my crew and I consisting of Mike Kenny, James Mong and Dave Hathaway were picked to travel to Langley AFB, Virginia to being training on the newest Air Force fighter aircraft, the F-15 Eagle that would replace the F-4 at Bitburg that summer. This training was about 3 months long and was quite the honor as we were the first crew from Bitburg to be trained there. The downside of being gone that long was that my son Jesse kind of forgot me and was pretty standoffish for a day or two following my return!

The F-15 was a sports car compared to the "family truckster" that the F-4 was. It carried only 3 weapons, AIM-9 heat seeking missiles, AIM-7 radar guided missiles and an internal 20mm Gatling gun. Easy to train on and simple to maintain. What a change and we all loved it! I would spend my remaining time at Bitburg leading the load crew training program in the 36th Munitions Maintenance Squadron.

On January 6th in 1979 our daughter Brandy was born in the German hospital (Krankenhaus) in the town of Bitburg. The delivery doctor was Iranian, the nurses were German and we couldn't hardly understand any of them! It all went well though and our family was now complete.

In the meantime I had heard about a five year stabilized assignment to Grand Forks AFB, North Dakota and though that would be good for us to be close to family. So I applied for it and soon after, received orders for there. I guess not many others wanted to go to the cold part of the country so it was readily available to me. We were thrilled about it.

My assignment there wasn't supposed to start until August of that year but Deb's dad Don had suffered a stroke and died in March and since I already had my orders for Grand Forks I asked to go there early in conjunction with emergency leave. It was denied by my First Sergeant,

Merriweather Lewis, a direct descendant of THE Merriweather Lewis by the way, who also told me that I couldn't even go on emergency leave because my father-in-law wasn't immediate family!

He was wrong and I talked to my neighbor Pete Bailey about it. He called the Senior Enlisted Advisor, CM Sgt Brown, who talked to his boss General Perry Smith, the 36th TFW commander. Soon after that I was told to report to the General's office along with First Sergeant Lewis and CM Sgt Brown.

After hearing the facts General Smith then told me that I would get emergency leave but since the Wing was preparing for an Operational Readiness Inspection that I had to return because of the need for experienced people for it. He then gave the following direct order to Sergeant Lewis; you will complete emergency leave paperwork for Sergeant Gilbertson, you will arrange for him to get any funds he needs from the Credit Union, even if they are closed (they were) and you will personally arrange transportation for Sergeant Gilbertson and his family to the airport in Frankfurt! Needless to say, the General was sure pissed off with Sergeant Lewis!

So then I had to endure the wrath of him in the orderly room while he was banging out paperwork on a typewriter because he was pissed off at me! At one point he demanded to see a copy of my Grand Forks orders and then did some more typing and finally tore that sheet out and took it into the executive officer, Capt. Beard, for her signature since our Squadron commander was on leave. She really didn't understand what she was signing as she wasn't aware of the facts and it wasn't leave paperwork at all but was travel orders to report to Grand Forks AFB following my leave time!

This was Sergeant Lewis' way of getting back at the General for the ass-chewing and I wasn't going to argue with him as I wanted to go to Grand Forks early! Even though I was told to be back I now had official orders telling me I didn't have to.

I then got a power of attorney for Pete Bailey to arrange for pack up and shipping of our household stuff and that evening we left Germany for home.

Chapter 28

Grand Forks AFB, North Dakota

I arrived at the Minneapolis Airport about an hour after Deb and the kids with Deb's brother Steve and his wife Sharon there to meet us. We had arrived in a blizzard and so Highway 12 was closed in Dassel so we had to spend several hours in the Norseman Café there until the highway was plowed open. It was good to be with family again but unfortunately it was the death of Deb's dad to bring us all together again. He was only 58 and it was such a shock to everyone.

After our return, I took a month's leave and then left for Grand Forks to sign in while Deb stayed with her mom with the kids. It was back to B-52s again but this time it was in a nuclear Cold War environment instead of the conventional weapons mission in Thailand. I applied for and got quarters in base housing and as soon as we could move in I brought Deb and kids up there to set up house.

We stayed in base housing about a year until we bought our first house at 619 13th Ave South in Grand Forks. We really liked living there for the 6 years we were there with the best part being our closeness to our families so our kids Jesse and Brandy knew their grandparents, aunts, uncles and cousins and that has been their benefit to this day.

Jesse, Deb, Brandy and me in North Dakota

I was back on the B-52 but this time the mission of the 319th Bomb Wing was nuclear deterrence so my job as a weapons load crew chief was somewhat different than what I experienced in Thailand.

The winter months were on the severe end at times and even more so when working out on the flight line for an eight hour shift in minus 40 or colder temperatures. We learned very fast to stay away from forced air heaters out there because once any time was spent in front of one to warm up it was near impossible to leave it and get back to the severe cold! So it was better to stay cold until relieved. As long as we wore our Artic parkas, pants and "bunny boots" we were fine.

The 319th Bomb Wing nuclear commitment was with gravity bombs, SRAM (Short Range Attack Missiles) and ALCM (Air Launched Cruise Missiles) and a certain number of B-52s were kept fully loaded and ready for instant take-off from the high security alert pad with the same number of KC-135 tanker aircraft if the "horn" ever sounded. God forbid!

Besides our constant training requirements each month, the alert pad was where we did our most critical work. Before a B-52 was taken off alert a replacement had to be towed there and fully uploaded and functional checked and be declared fully operational before the B-52 it replaced could be taken off alert and downloaded. At no time could our alert force have less than the designated number of aircraft on full alert.

After being a crew chief for a year I was elevated to shift supervisor. Then about a year after that I had to take my turn on an involuntary assignment to Bomb Wing HQ as a Weapons Quality Control inspector. A job I hated because this group was dominated by aircraft maintenance people who gave us weapons guys no support in our duties but constantly tasked us to know and even perform theirs which we weren't qualified to do. It was by far the most distasteful work environment I had experienced in my Air Force career.

A year and a half later I was finally assigned back to the 319th Munitions Squadron as the NCOIC of the Weapons Loading section and back to what I knew best. I was now responsible for the "care and feeding" of 50 or so junior airmen which is quite the challenge but I was happy for it.

While at Grand Forks I finally reasoned that more education would be of a benefit to my Air Force career so I enrolled at the University of North Dakota and took night classes. I guess the saying, "what doesn't kill you makes you stronger" influenced it. Really? Anyway I soon came to realize that I had developed near "zero" study habits in high school so it was a real challenge.

I guess the main benefit of my enrollment at UND was hockey tickets and not education. Hockey at UND is akin to another religion and its popularity there is unbelievable. It was near impossible to get tickets for their home games but with my student ID we had no problem so we got into the hockey spirit while in Grand Forks. The UND Fighting Sioux were perennially the number one team in the nation or close to it so the games were always very exciting, especially when they played the Minnesota Gophers.

I also had to have reconstructive surgery on my elbow soon after arrival there. This stemmed from an injury received in Germany from either lifting missiles or weights in the gym. It got so bad I couldn't pick Brandy up but had to have Deb hand her to me. After numerous cortisone injections, which didn't work, I finally was referred to an orthopedic specialist who recommended surgery so off I went to Fitzsimmons Army Hospital in Denver, Colorado to have it done. Surgery was a success and I was back to normal after surgery.

I also took a part-time job as an orderly in a nursing home in Grand Forks and what a rewarding experience it was. It was wonderful working with the elderly who couldn't be alone. It is a service everyone should experience.

And after 6 years there I got a phone call from a good friend of mine from previous assignment, Ed Richards, who asked me if I would consider an assignment to Ramstein AB, Germany, where he was stationed. So Deb and I talked it over and decided that we needed another life change and so decided to go there. Ed was pretty tight with the weapons assignments people there and so a month later I received orders to report to the 86th Air Generation Squadron in the fall of 1985.

I had also bought a new 1984 Harley Davidson Sportster while at Grand Forks, AFB but sold it years later in Missouri before Jesse was old enough to drive it.

Promotion wise, Grand Forks AFB was good for me as I arrived there as a Staff Sergeant and left there as a Master Sergeant

Chapter 29

Ramstein Air Base, Germany

At NCO Academy, Kapaun AB, Germany 1986

On arrival at Rhein Main AB outside of Frankfurt we were met by Ed and his wife Linda for the trip to Ramstein AB. I was stationed with Ed at Utapao, Thailand and then at Bitburg, Germany with him, Linda and their 3 sons Kenny, Brian, and Michael so we were good friends. Ed loaned us their second car to use till we got our own so we had wheels while we checked out a number of potential places to rent on the economy while we waited for on-base housing.

We finally settled on the lower floor of a new house owned by Jürgen and Elke Barnack in the village of Steinbach, about 10 miles from Ramstein. They and their two children Jens and Sondra lived in the upper level and we adapted to each other easily. Jesse and Brandy played with their kids a lot and they also had a big German Shepard named Asta that finally accepted us also. We loved living in that village as it was so quiet, the people were friendly to us, and the local countryside was beautiful and great for long walks.

During the Christmas season there were festivals in many of the local villages where the main fare was bratwursts and "Gluhwein" which was a hot spiced wine, and very good! Sometimes too good! And in our village, the American residents would gather together and go around the village and sing Christmas carols for many of the older Germans.

We all had a great time as when we finished singing at a house, out they would come with glasses of schnapps as thanks! So for us who partook of a glass, it didn't take many stops before our signing took on a more robust pitch! The locals really cherished this of us and we really enjoyed doing it.

My assignment was with the 86th AGS (Aircraft Generation Squadron) as the assistant NCOIC of the weapons loading section. Though the 86th TFW (Tactical Fighter Wing) flew the old F-4, we were awaiting the arrival and changeover to the new F-16C fighter and that is what I was assigned to so I didn't have anything to do with the F-4, thank god!

For about a month I went to school to learn the F-16 armament systems and not long after we started receiving them, four at a time. The F-16, like the F-15, was also a joy to work with.

After a year there, I received orders to attend the NCO (Non-Commissioned Officer's) Academy at Kapaun Air Station. This was a 6 week in-residence school about 8 miles from Ramstein so I wasn't far from home. Upon graduation, I was to be the NCOIC of the loading section as my boss had left for another job and at that time I was also offered a job at the headquarters of USAFE (U.S. Air Forces in Europe), stationed at Ramstein.

Now I had a decision to make, but the idea of doing something completely new won out so I accepted this new assignment and not long after, processed out of the 86th AGS and into HQUSAFE/LGWRP, which shortened was that I was now the Requirements and Plans "worker bee" in the Logistics and Weapons Division!

A sampling of my new job taskings were to monitor maintenance and storage issues of weapons and support equipment pre-positioned throughout Europe and armament issues relative to wartime basing requirements for stateside fighter wings in case the "cold war" went hot! The boss in my office was a Major and there were three Captains and a Senior M.Sgt.

One of my main taskings was to negotiate and set up munitions requirements for stateside fighter squadrons for their wartime training at their forward operating bases throughout Europe. This allowed me to travel to these locations and to meet with their advance planning team to work out their needs.

These week long trips took me to England several times, to the Netherlands, various locations in Germany and three places in Turkey. Obviously, these taskings were my favorite part of my job as I got to experience these very different and sometimes unusual locations. Turkey was, by far, my favorite of them all.

Among the places we travelled to as a family when either my parents or Deb's mom came over for a visit were Denmark, Norway, where we stayed with my relatives Pal and Lise Tallakson for several days and Mom and Dad with Bjorn and Rigmar Tallakson, Mom's cousin. Then through Sweden and back. Also many places throughout Germany and the Netherlands. With Deb's mom Shirley we went to Yugoslavia for a week on the Adriatic coast and then Sarajevo but didn't really enjoy that trip as much as Yugoslavia was still under communist control so we had to turn in our passports wherever we stayed and were even followed while in Sarajevo!

Our first day there and while out walking and visiting various retail stores I finally noticed that there was a guy that was always a short distance behind us and stopped when we stopped to window shop or enter a store. The next morning I went down to the front desk for something and behind the desk was this same guy talking to the clerk! As soon as he saw me he took off running out the door!

Even entering the country we were hassled by the border guards and so as interesting our time was in Yugoslavia I couldn't wait to leave it.

I will regress here back to the day we first entered Yugoslavia and what set the tone for our visit there. When we arrived at the border crossing to get our passports stamped and gave them to the very unfriendly guard, we were directed to pull off to the side of the guard shack and wait. We waited and waited and after about an hour I finally went inside to ask about our passports.

The guard pointed to a back room and at a table were four guards playing cards while our passports were laying on the table corner. When I asked if they were stamped, a guard picked them up and half threw them to me and was laughing about it with the other guards. I was furious but bit my tongue, walked out and drove off for the rest of our nervous time there. What a relief to finally cross the border into Austria and FREEDOM!

We did have one enjoyable experience there though when we stayed for several days in the small town of Makarska on the Adriatic coast. The local tourist agent contacted a local guy by the name of Branko Borkovic who lived with his mother and they had a couple of bedrooms in their house for us to stay in. they were so nice and even made several meals for us.

We really loved our time living in Steinbach but with my change of job going to USAFE Headquarters and the requirement to travel around Europe in support of stateside units we thought it best to live on base where family support would be better for Deb and the kids during my absences.

While we still lived in Steinbach though and when my parents were visiting us we by accident discovered that anti-Semitism was still prevalent there. We were on a walk through the hills around Steinbach one morning when we came upon a fenced off cemetery overgrown with weeds and with an "Eintritte Verboten" (entry forbidden) sign on the locked gate. We could see Jewish writing on the grave stones and that pissed me off so I forced the locked gate open and in we went.

At one time there had to have been a sizable Jewish community there as some of the later deaths were in the early 1900's and it was also a good sized cemetery. Where they went and why was probably no great mystery being in Germany but then I felt that I's better not ask either. The Germans were real big on honoring the dead with beautiful picturesque cemeteries and then to see this rundown unkempt one had to be a reflection of past and continuing prejudice. Anyway, that's how I saw it.

One of our last trips before leaving Germany was to Italy for a week on the beach. We drove down to Rimini on the Adriatic coast and stayed in the Levante Hotel with the beach just across the road. Since going topless was pretty much the norm on the beaches there, Jesse and Brandy had a great time running around and counting the topless women until they finally tired of it in a couple of days and then it was no big deal. While there we took a day trip by bus to the tiny country of San Marino that is completely encircled by Italy. It was interesting to be in another country that was about the size of a small town.

Deb and I on the beach in Rimini, Italy 1987

Deb and I in a wheat field above our home in Steinbach, Germany 1985

Since my time in Germany was just about up I needed to consider where to go next when it so happened that there was a need for a Weapons Systems MSgt to be the armament superintendent on a site activation task force at Whiteman AFB, Missouri, which was to be the future home of the new B-2 bomber. CMsgt Dick Vancil the head 462 at HQUSAFE/LGW and also a good friend first heard about it from his counterpart at HQ Sac at Offutt AFB, Nebraska. Since this was a recommendation assignment only and not open to just anyone, Chief Vancil politicked for me and not much later I received the assignment there. My job experience at headquarters was a definite plus but to be recommended for this unique position was a great honor for which I did not take lightly and of which I still am grateful for.

Since my assignment to Whiteman AFB didn't go through the normal assignment process, about a month later I received another assignment to George AFB California near the town of Victorville in the high desert. What? After about a week of phone calls by myself and Chief Vancil and HQ SAC to the Air Force assignments section, George AFB was cancelled and I would be off to Missouri.

We were to leave Germany the first week in September of 1988 but on the 28th of August we were eye witness to one of the worst air show disasters to ever happen on an Air Force base. Ramstein was host to the annual Flugtag airshow where the entry gates were open to the public.

About 300,000 people, mostly Germans, were in attendance to view the various military aircraft on static display and to watch the many aerial demonstration teams from different countries perform overhead.

Since all our furniture had been packed and shipped to Missouri we had not much else to so we spent most of the day at the airshow. At about 4:00 PM the Frecce Tricolor demonstration team from Italy was performing their aerial maneuvers when one of the jets collided with two others head-on and crashed into the huge crowd near the runway killing 46 people. It came down and impacted in a ball of flame and many more were killed from the burning jet fuel and others by parts of the exploding jets.

Deb, Brandy and I were over on the flight line wandering amongst the various jets on display about a quarter mile from the crash site but were watching the planes when they collided. Mass chaos started with people screaming, leaving and running to get away as far away as possible. We had no idea where Jesse was but knew that he had been hanging around the Boy Scout tent that was in the vicinity of the crash site so needless to say we were frantic with worry but couldn't get near there against the rush of thousands of people running from there. Security Police were evacuating everyone but emergency personnel so the only thing we could do was walk home and wait. There was instant relief for us when we walked up to our apartment and there was Jesse!

The rest of the day and night was just awful with ambulance sirens and helicopters coming and going all night and even the next day. The two main gates were closed down to allow only emergency medical use so there were several hundred thousand Europeans that couldn't go home and didn't have military identification. All communication systems were also closed down so we couldn't talk to our families back home who had heard the news but couldn't contact us and were also frantic with worry. After a couple of days we finally got through to them to tell them we were all right.

The next day while I was out processing prior to leaving Germany I ran into a co-worker from my days on the flight line and he told me he laid flat on the ground as the burning jet bounced over him and landed in a crowd of people where most of the deaths occurred. He was still in shock too while describing the scene, the victims and his attempts to help them.

Chapter 30

Whiteman AFB, Missouri

Our Family, Allen, Brandy, Jesse and Deb

After an uneventful flight from Frankfurt, Germany to Minneapolis, Minnesota we were picked up at the airport by my brother Lynn and we stayed with him for several days in St Michael while I looked for a car. I settled on a 1984 Honda Accord and the drove down to Litchfield and Montevideo to spend time with our families before leaving for Missouri. It was great to get reacquainted with our families after being away for three years.

After a nine hour drive we arrived at the main gate that was surprisingly a small guard shack with a maybe 100 watt light bulb shining on us. What a shock to experience the difference of larger Air Force bases versus a smaller strategic missile base of what Whiteman AFB currently was. After having to explain to the guard why I was there I was give directions to the billeting office to check in and get me temporary quarters until we found permanent housing.

I had called the billeting office that morning to confirm our arrival that evening and they assured me that we would have newly built temporary quarters with 2 bedrooms and a kitchen, etc. for 30 days. When we got there those quarters were no longer available even though I had reserved them. We would be housed in a re-conditioned old barracks until the new place was available. So we went there and opened the door to cockroaches scurrying about when I turned the light on. What? But the worst was when we opened the refrigerator and it was like a roach stampede.

After I quick exit to the car and back to the office to complain to deaf ears, we were given a different unit and we only had a couple roaches there. Ha! So we toughed it out for two days until new quarters were ours for the next 30 days.

The stigma surrounding cockroaches was well warranted as they were truly nasty creatures but were also a source of entertainment having dealt with them over the years of living in the southern states and in Thailand. There were countless ways to torment them and to dispatch them and in this task I was an expert.

When I was stationed at Utapao AB Thailand and Deb came there to live for a time we were, "blessed" with a small Gecko lizard that hung out on the coffee table in our bungalow. We also were blessed with a number of large cockroaches and when one would come out of hiding the little lizard would immediately attack it and fight it off back into hiding. That was sure fun to watch!

Another indication of how small and quiet base this was when we went to the non-commissioned officers club to eat and we were the only customers. When we were seated and ordered our meals they rolled out the salad bar for us. When were finished and paid the bill they rolled the salad bar back into the kitchen again and turned the lights off.

The next day I checked into the B-2 Site Activation Task Force (SATAF) where I would work for the next eight years. My new boss was Colonel Skip O'Hara and I also met most of my co-workers all who were the top in their respective fields and all self-starters. I was very welcomed into the fold and couldn't wait to start work with these fellow airmen.

My job title was the B-2 Armament System Superintendent and I would be responsible for field activation of Whiteman AFB to receive the new B-2 weapon system. I would be responsible for acquisition of all armament support equipment and for reviewing of the design plans and construction of munitions support facilities and to plan and coordinate installation of the Weapons load trainer which was basically a B-2 aircraft that couldn't fly. It was an aircraft mockup with all the real aircraft armaments systems for weapons load crews to train on and was the first of its kind in the Air Force.

Along with the responsibilities came numerous trips to the Boeing plant in Seattle and the Northrup B-2 division in Pico Rivera, a suburb of Los Angeles, CA. where I presented our munition and armament related issues to the builders and contractors at ongoing meetings for the next several years.

At first I felt that I was way in over my head with all these experts dealing with issues that were way above my pay grade. I soon came to an understanding though on how to deal with our issues face to face with Air Force requirements the priority, as the end user.

We started house hunting immediately as we didn't want to live on base. With the recommendation of our new banker we went with Rick Reith as our realtor. He was a single guy in his 30s and was a lot of fun to house hunt with. We looked at numerous houses in the surrounding area and finally settled on a house at 819 East Market in Warrensburg. Its only drawback was that railroad tracks were one block away but the times we looked at the house there were no trains going through.

Rick assured us that there were only several trains per day but after the first day and night in our new home we counted sixteen trains. What the Hell? I believe that he knew the train schedules and only showed us the house when he knew there wouldn't be any trains. Ha! I guess we got suckered. It took a while to get used to the trains at night but then later it only bothered us when relatives came to visit as I know it kept them awake at night.

We also experienced first-hand when we went carpet shopping that racism was alive and well in Warrensburg. We were looking at carpet samples in a downtown store when the sales person asked our address. Our house was on East Market but we mistakenly said West Market. The sales gal said, with a surprised look, "Oh! So you live out there with all those colored people." WTF? So out the door we walked to another carpet store. We experienced a number of issues like that during our years in Missouri.

After having getting caught up in the race issues involving the Martin Luther King assassination while traveling back to Florida through the Atlanta airport in 1968 I was also caught up in the Rodney King rioting while on a business trip to Los Angeles during that awful time. After a long day of meetings with Northrup engineers I was out eating in some restaurant in Whittier when a police officer came in and told everyone to leave immediately as rioters were only several blocks away.

I left my meal and went back to the hotel. From the top floor of the hotel I watched the fires all over the L.A. basin as the rioting was sprawling city wide. Luckily I was flying out of the Ontario airport which was west of Los Angeles so I had no problem getting out the next day. Because of the rioting most roads to the LA airport were closed so a number of my fellow meeting attendees couldn't leave until the rioting was suppressed.

Along with the ongoing Logistics Working Group meeting in Los Angeles and Armament Systems Quarterly Reviews in Seattle I was routinely gone to Fort Worth, Texas, Oklahoma City, Wichita, Kansas, Wright –Patterson AFB, Ohio, Eglin AFB, Florida and less often to other locales. As often as I travelled though, some of my co-workers were TDY on average of two weeks every month so I was fortunate in that regard.

Deb took a job as the health aide at the Warrensburg Middle school and along with that was a free pass for us to all the high school sporting events so we went to most football, basketball and volleyball home games. Warrensburg had great teams every year in all the sports so they had a good fan base and always filled the bleachers. That was so much fun and to this day we still attend most home basketball games in New London.

I had dabbled in the sport of tennis in previous years and had a great desire to play at it but I sucked at it terribly even though playing a lot in Grand Forks and in Germany. I had never learned the correct strokes and strategy so that led to a lack of interest until a conversation with my second in command at SATAF, Col. Tom Hoskins one day. Tennis came up in the conversation and when he said he was a USTA (United States Tennis Association) teaching pro and would I like to hit the court with him. I was hooked.

I was an eager student so we were on a tennis court during noon lunch almost every day. Col. Hoskins spent a lot of time working on my weak areas and soon I would be able to hold my own against him, mostly although he always kicked my ass! It never frustrated me though and several years later it would be a toss-up on which one of us won a match. Several nights a week we met at the Warrensburg city courts for a three set match and whether the match was two hours long or three hours we always had a battle and I loved it. Every Saturday even into winter I played doubles with a number of local players from Warrensburg from 8:00 AM to sometimes 1:00 PM. I also played in a city intramural league. Col. Hoskins and I also played each in Los Angles if we were TDY together and I even entered a small tournament there but got beat by a teenager.

As a Senior Msgt I was due to attend the Senior NCO Academy in Montgomery, Alabama which was a two month in-residence course. As I detested school so much I had used the importance of my job as an excuse to not go. Now that I was down to the final year of eligibility for promotion to Chief Msgt, it was either attend or retire so I went.

Overall it was a good two months. I learned a lot and came back from it more at ease speaking in front of a group. This would really pay off in my future and pay off it did. That fall while at a meeting in Seattle with Boeing engineers it was announced that I had just been promoted to Chief Master Sergeant. Now I would be in the elite one percent of the Air Force. The rest of the day was a blur and after much congrats, back slapping and "attaboys," I went back to the hotel, called up a friend who lived in Tacoma and gave him the news. He drove over and we celebrated into the night at a bar next door!

After my return home there were more celebrations but I still had to wait until my promotion sequence number came up. In May of 1993 I sewed on the stripe and then was official. Within the year I received a "request" from HQ USAF to go to Dhahran, Saudi Arabia to serve as the 4404th Fighter Wing Weapons Manager in support of

Desert Storm and Southern Watch for a 90 day rotation. Since it was considered the "death knell" to a career to turn down a "request" from higher headquarters, I took the assignment so it was off to the desert in March for 90 plus days.

Chapter 31

King Abdul Aziz Air Base, Dhahran, Saudi Arabia

I flew out of Kansas City to Philadelphia on the 28th of February and there waited for the flight to Germany and then on to Saudi Arabia. I was because my rank, afforded VIP status and to my surprise a flight attendant tracked me down and escorted me across the terminal to the VIP lounge! What? That lasted one free drink as I felt so out of place in there with real VIPs. So I went back to the departure terminal to be with fellow Air Force people and was pretty much left alone there to because of my rank. I was irritated to the point of being angry that I so intimidated others but that's just what it was.

When we boarded the plane I was given the first seat in first class and that didn't sit well with some of the officers who had to sit back in coach with the enlisted people. I heard a few comments from a Major and some Captains as to how I rated the number one seat but they also knew that I had a higher status than them, I was on the same level as a Colonel so I paid them no mind.

After about 15 hours in the air and after a stopover at Rhein Main AB, Germany we finally landed in Saudi Arabia. After getting baggage that was all searched for contraband and porn, I met up with CMsgt Randy Creech who I was to replace. He got me settled in to my dorm room and that's the last I saw of him as he flew out on the plane I came in on. I slept for about an hour after two days of no sleep and then got up to process in and start work. My new desert camouflage uniforms were in my room when I got there so I was ready to go. I was in a suite along with the First Sergeant so I had it good while I was there. We had a common kitchen, our own separate bedrooms and bathrooms and my own car assigned to me.

Of immediate notice upon arrival was the extreme heat and with close proximity to the Persian Gulf it was also more humid especially after dark. I kept a record of the temperatures during the 92 days I was there and it was never below 100 degrees. The hottest day I recorded was 118 degrees in the shade! And since alcohol was forbidden in the Kingdom there was no cold beer at the end of the day.

Nighttime was the best time for jogging since it was slightly cooler but that was when the civil engineers sprayed for mosquitoes and there was a constant white fog in the air. There was no way I would breathe that in so my fitness was maintained in the gym and weight room. Since there wasn't much to do over there when not at work I spent a lot of time in the gym.

One of my "things" was treating myself to a Snickers candy bar every day but then I had to work it off on the stair stepper machine burning off the 120 calories of the candy bar. I did that religiously plus weight lifting and it was sure a good time killer.

My job there would be my first time as a Wing Weapons Manager and with no real turnover from my predecessor I had to learn on the fly. My first day at work I was informed I had to chair a weekly meeting with the fighter and munitions squads to resolve differences and problem areas that seemed to happen on a daily if not hourly rate between them. I was proud of the fact that I never had to use the power of my rank or position to resolve disputes. My leadership was more as a moderator leading them to a mutual resolution in which they were all satisfied. When not in meetings my average day was spent visiting all the various fighter squadron armament sections, weapons release shops and gun shops. If they were lacking in any support or equipment needed I made sure they got it and worked to resolve any issues they had with other units.

The fighter squadrons were sent there on 90 day rotations so every month there was a new squadron that needed transition to a wartime setting. There was a marked difference in the way stateside fighter squadrons conducted their routine missions to what they were to experience on their arrival in Saudi Arabia. Even though they trained for wartime they had to learn our way of doing things so it was challenging in that regard.

In my 92 days in Saudi Arabia I only took one day off and that didn't even last the whole day as I was so bored hanging around the apartment that I uniformed up and went back to the flight line. Operations there were on a 24/7 schedule so I could always be busy. Working made the time pass much faster.

Occasionally in the evening my office mate MSgt Krause would go to one of the two malls in Dhahran. The Saudi mall was unlike any mall I had ever seen. It was made almost of all marble with gold plating. Most of the stores were like the super high dollar stores seen on Rodeo Drive in Los Angeles or in New York (Prada, Fendi). We never saw customers in there as the Saudi women did all of their shopping in them after closing in keeping with their religion I was told. There also wasn't much people watching either as the Saudi men were all dressed in their white robes and the women were in all black with everything covered but their eyes.

There would be young Saudi boys flirting with young Saudi girls and we always wondered if the boys really knew what the girls looked like when all they saw was their eyes. I guessed they must have.

There was another mall farther into the city and this was mainly for the third country nationals who were brought into Saudi Arabia to perform the menial labor for the Saudis. We preferred this mall as it was a lower to middle class mall with many common retailers that we could afford to deal with. Just the drive down to the mall was a scary ordeal as most Saudis had cars but they also paid no attention to any rules of the road. Most of them were basically second generation camel herders who had become rich from oil. They believed that turning the lights on after dark would ruin the car battery so they drove without lights. It was constant to either meet a dark oncoming car or be passed by one. Our term for that was, "They are on the road to Allah." At least they could see us.

This is kind of a humorous joke but also not a joke. We had to drive like this. Too dangerous not to.

KINGDOM OF SAUDI ARABIA

RULES OF THE ROAD
(As observed)

Right-of-way Rules:

1. You have the Right-of-way in all situations.

2. If anyone ever infringes on your Right-of-way, honk your horn at the offender and gesticulate wildly.

3. Yeild the Right-of-way when it amuses you. For example, you might wish to yeild to a large truck with "Ben-Hur" style hubcaps that threatens to knock your spokes out.

Traffic Signs and Signals:

1. Traffic signs are informative and decorative only.

2. Traffic signal lights take precedence over signs, especially in decorative value. The following rules are optional:
    a. Red Light - stopping is permitted
    b. Right turn on red light is permitted
    c. Left turn on red light is permitted
    d. Straight ahead on red light is permitted
    e. Green light means honk your horn and go. Honking your horn serves three basic purposes:
        (1) It announces that the light has changed to drivers who have crept half way through the intersection already.
        (2) It wakes the driver in front of you
        (3) It proves that you're not asleep
    f. Yellow light has no meaning

Turning and Passing:

1. Passing is permitted anywhere. Intersections, on/off ramps, road shoulders, and sidewalks are all good examples of places to pass cars that impede your progress.

2. Lane markers are decorative only. Make efficient use of all the road's surface by straddling lane markers or creating temporary lanes wherever your vehicle will fit. Note: A car is about as wide as a camel.

3. Perform the following actions when turning:

    a. Announce your intention to turn by staring straight ahead

I constantly observed this behavior when driving to and from the city of Dhahran and had to adjust to it!

      b. Before turning right, move to the extreme left of the road
      c. Before turning left, move to the extreme right of the road
      d. If any vehicles are between you and your destination while turning, honk your horn and execute a palm down shoo-ing' gesture at them.

  4. Perform the following actions when passing:

      a. Come up as close as possible behind the car in front of you. During hours of darkness, flash your high beams. Driving with lights off or parking lights only increases the contrast when you flash your high beams at night
      b. If the vehicle ahead does not immediately move over or drive off the road, announce your intention to pass by staring straight ahead and swerving to the side
      c. Pass only on the left regardless of how many lanes are open to the right. Use of the shoulder (also known as "The Road to Mecca") is permitted
      d. Disregard any oncoming traffic on two-way roads. They must yield as you have the Right-of-way!

Vehicle Lighting:

  1. Although the primary purpose of headlights is to warn drivers to get out of your way, headlights can also be used at night when it is too dark to see where your going. When it is not a very dark night or when driving on an illuminated freeway, headlights are unnecessary. It is a good idea to use parking lights in these situations.

  2. Use your emergency flashing lights in rain or dust storms. You may also use these lights while backing up on the highway.

  3. Turn signals are used by foreigners to demonstrate their ignorance of local driving customs and etiquette. Most turn signals are inoperative or cross-wired so they flash on the wrong side. It is safer not to use them at all.

  4. In the event that the turn signals are in working order, they serve two purposes:
      a. The right turn signal lets the driver behind you know that there is traffic coming
      b. The left turn signal lets the driver behind you know it is clear to pass

General Information:

  Always drive in the most unconventional, ill-advised, and inconsistent manner possible. Besides arousing or amusing responses from foreigners, constant reckless unpredictability is the only dedicated method to ensure other drivers will fully anticipate your next foolhardy move. This is the key to safe driving. Remember, "Driving is an art, a taste, and a courtesy."*

  * *A Driver's Guide for Careful and Safe Driving, Kingdom of Saudi Arabia, Ministry of the Interior, Public Security General Traffic Directorate.*

    The two page Rules of the Road letter was passed out to all personnel at our in-processing to the Air base and though it is rather comical, it was very correct as to the driving habits of the Saudis.

    There was only one tennis court out at the Oasis recreation area and I would drive out there quite a bit after work to hit against a rebound wall. I couldn't find any one to play against and the rebound wall got old pretty quickly. One night there were two guys playing on the court with one of them being pretty good and the other one not at all. I sat there and watched them play for a while until they quit and got ready to leave. The better player came up to me and asked if I had a partner who was coming to play. I told him, "No, just me and the wall." He said, "I'm here, let's hit."

We soon determined we were of pretty equal ability and could give each other some competition. He was an RF-4C pilot by the name of Captain Sammeniago and insisted I call him, "Sammy." We played each other 3 or 4 times a week at least and became good friends the rest of our time there. Our many games on the court sure helped pass the time quicker.

Saudi Arabia has one religion and it is the Wahhabi sect of Islam and is the strictest of the various branches of Islam. All alcohol is forbidden as is any material or item with images of a female with exposed skin above the ankles. Other religions are forbidden in the Kingdom so church services on the base were held in secret or at least not publicized. Their society I very much male dominated and that was witnessed routinely. I didn't hold them in high regard during my time there, I did respect though that they were very rigid in their centuries old customs and allowed no outside influences on their way of life.

Their legal system was such that any crime or criminal act was dealt with severely and quickly. Therefore there was very little crime in Saudi Arabia and what was committed was mostly by foreigners. Drug offenses and capital crimes meant an automatic death sentence that was usually to be carried out within 30 days by beheading in Riyadh, the capital city of Saudi Arabia. Not long before I was stationed there public beheadings were made off limits to American military personnel by the Saudi government due an incident by some Marines at an execution. Apparently when the head was chopped off, the Marines started their "Hoo-ah" cheers and this pissed off the Saudi government, hence the ban.

Stealing was still dealt with by removal of a hand or hands but was supposedly done surgically instead of with an axe so it was more humane. I guess there was really no humane to remove a head though. What would be the point?

Along with the fighter squadrons at the 4404th provisional wing at Dhahran, I also had oversight of an A-10 fighter squadron stationed at

Al Jaber AB Kuwait and so hopped on a C-130 cargo aircraft heading there to spend a couple days observing their operation. This Kuwaiti air base had been overran and occupied by the Iraqis during their takeover of Kuwait during the Gulf War. The Iraqis had parked/hidden their fighter aircraft in the huge hardened aircraft shelters at Al Jaber but this was to no avail as our F-111s targeted each shelter with a 2000 lb LGB(Laser Guided Bomb) and even 8 feet of reinforced concrete was no protection as everything and everyone inside was obliterated.

While touring around the base I had noticed that there were combat boots scattered on the ground all over the flight line area and was told that those boots had previously had Iraqi feet in them until the F-111s attacked! After seeing the aftermath of the destruction the Iraqi Army caused in Kuwait City and accounts of their torture, executions and rape of Kuwaitis during their occupation, then my belief was that justice was served! They only brought on their own demise.

Later that afternoon a couple of the squadron armament supervisors asked if I would like a tour of Kuwait City and, of course, I was up for that so off we went. I soon found out that driving habits were no different in Kuwait, as on the four lane road to Kuwait City there were four cars coming at us in all lanes! I thought this was going to be a head-on for some but our driver said no, the one in our lane will move over, which he finally did! It was like that, I guess, in most of the Middle East countries as I saw the same traffic behavior even on a visit to Bahrain! There just were no proper rules to go by and there were lots of traffic fatalities because of it.

After two days at Al Jabar AB, it was another C-130 plane back to Dhahran and my routine there. My typical day there would be to head to my office around 6:30, start the coffee maker for the other building occupants and then to the *Warrior's Den* chow hall about a quarter mile away for breakfast. Then to probably a meeting or two, and visits to the fighter squadrons and, or, the weapons release shop, and, or the gun shop. Noon lunch was had back at the *Warrior's Den* and then more meetings and flight line checks the rest of the afternoon.

When my work day was done around four or five pm it was back to my quarters to change clothes for either the gym to lift weights or do the stair-stepper or to go and play tennis. Then back to shower and dress for the evening meal at the Desert Rose Chow hall on the main base. Then maybe to the small library or back to my quarters to either watch some news on a Saudi English speaking TV channel or read until bedtime. It was pretty much like that most every day there so was a treat to go downtown to a mall occasionally to break the monotony.

There was also a coalition French fighter squadron on the base but their only reason to even be there was to keep an eye on us, or at least that was the popular belief! They only flew about 10-15 southern watch sorties a month compared to our 200-300 so they were kind of a joke!

My time there was finally coming to the end and after putting in a full work day on my last day, it was a quick packing job and off to the departure terminal for my flight out on the "rotator" passenger plane to Germany. I did manage to have a short "turn over" discussion with my replacement through a chain-link fence as he was deplaning and I was preparing to board!

Not long after I left there a truck bomb was exploded outside one of our dormitories in Khobar Towers killing and injuring many of the Air Force members from the 33rd TFW from Eglin AFB. I knew a number of the weapons guys from my days there and two of them were among those killed.

I wasn't in Saudi Arabia during Desert Storm, the coalition operation that removed Sadaam Hussein's army and air force from Kuwait, but one of my co-workers at Grand Forks, John Oelshlager was killed there when the C-130 gunship he was an aircrew member was on was shot down in the Persian Gulf by a surface to air missile.

John wanted to do something different in our career field so he cross-trained to be a gun and cannon loader/maintainer on the gunship. These planes were meant to operate only in the darkness but the pilot elected to stay over target longer so the plane became visible at first light, was seen and was destroyed. This was another case of senseless death due to pilot error. John was one of my favorite people and "saved" me from a toss into the river by drunken co-workers at my farewell party in Grand Forks!

Chapter 32

Back to Whiteman AFB

*At my going away party from the B-2 SATAF. I had just
returned from Saudi Arabia and was very tan.*

Upon my return from Saudi Arabia I was next to be the weapons manager of the 509th bomb wing. My friend Bob Davis, a fellow chief who was the current weapons manager was retiring and with my position at the SATAF going away as the B-2 was becoming operational, I was next in line as I was already on station. So after a SATAF farewell party I only had to walk "across the street" to my new position in the bomb wing.

Since I was now the Air Force focal point for B-2 weapons training my main responsibility was to oversee training and maintainability of the B-2 WLT (Weapons Load Trainer). It was basically a B-2 without wings and had only the mechanical and electrical systems required by weapons personnel in it. Needless to say, since access to an operational B-2 was restricted, the WLT and its training facility were a main attraction for tour groups to the base.

The new facility it was housed in had a white acrylic finished floor and the floor alongside the walls were lined with the simulated training weapons that the load crews trained on, with the exception of classified items. It was a "showplace" and because of that our training schedule was routinely disrupted in order to accommodate a tour group, whether it be military or civilian VIPs.

Most of the time I would get a day or two advance notice of an upcoming tour and would adjust accordingly but occasionally would get a call from either General Marcotte or his secretary to get ready to give a tour and briefing to either high ranking generals or some senator or Congress person! And an hours' notice was usually the case with these VIPs so there the scramble started to stop training and spiff up everything and prepare the briefing, based on the audience!

General Marcotte, the 509th bomb wing commander insisted that I briefed these VIPs because of my rank but for most other tour groups I would have one of my trainers, Technical SGT Patsy Metz, give the briefings.

Because of the extra secrecy of the B-2 and the classified weapons system inherent to it, I and my personnel had top secret level three security clearances. This meant that OSI (Office of Special Investigations) agents completed a background check on each of us to include interviewing neighbors, friends and relatives about us that went back years in the past, to ensure that we weren't crazy or drug addicts or criminals! When I and my standardization crew were tasked by the air force to conduct testing and physical fit testing of a new highly classified weapon, we had to be upgraded to a level four clearance and so had to go through an ever more intense background check.

Right before the weapon was to be delivered I got a call from the B-2 program office at Wright-Patterson AFB, Illinois that one of my guys had his security clearance pulled and that testing was put on hold until a replacement could be cleared and trained. What? The reason was that he missed a college loan payment before he enlisted in the Air Force! That's how technical our background checks were conducted! So I said "bullshit," and elevated it through my chain of command, got General Marcotte involved in the issue and several days later my guy was cleared and good to go. The testing went as scheduled and was successfully completed. To this day I believe that particular weapon is still top secret!

Rumors were coming down the Air Force rumor mill that HQ USAF was going to implement a new program air force wide that was called the "Ready Chief" program. Its objective was to move us chiefs that had been on station for more than six years to a new assignment to better spread our expertise at other bases with different missions. Since I had been at Whiteman AFB eight years, but in two different positions, I knew that it would affect me and sure enough, I got a call from General Marcotte's secretary for a meeting with him.

So he informed me personally that he could not justify to HQ USAF to keep me there because of my lengthy time and asked me for a recommended replacement, which I gave and he agreed with so I was at least good with that. I really didn't want to leave my job there but knew it was time and I could have retired then but at least wanted to know what my new assignment possibilities were. The two bases that HQ USAF gave me a choice of were Cannon AFB, New Mexico and Hill AFB, Utah!

I had been to Cannon AFB on a TDY years earlier and never wanted to see that place ever again and Hill AFB was in Ogden Utah and close to a lot of skiing so the choice was obvious! And so I soon received my new orders to report to Hill AFB as the 388th Fighter Wing Weapons Manager, reporting in October of 1996.

I also had purchased a 1968 Plymouth Roadrunner muscle car while in Missouri and was such a cool car but didn't want to drive it to Utah so I sold it. That was one car I should have kept because the value of something like that has skyrocketed over the years. Hindsight!!

My 1968 Plymouth Roadrunner

Chapter 33

Hill AFB, Utah

After several farewell parties put on by armament personnel from the 393rd Bomb Squadron, the Whiteman Chiefs Group and the 509th Operations Group, I out-processed the base and left on the 30th of September 1996 for Utah.

Having spent that night in Billeting at FE Warren AFB in Cheyenne, Wyoming, I arrived at Hill AFB the next afternoon and signed in and was assigned Chiefs quarters for a month until I could arrange for on-base quarters or a house off base.

After reporting to my new boss Colonel Steven Bozarth, and meeting some of the weapons people I would be in charge of I promptly "gave" myself ten days off for house hunting, met with a realtor and found the perfect, fairly new house in South Ogden, about a 15-minute drive from the base. Deb, still being back in Missouri was pretty skeptical about me buying our next home without her there too but after seeing pictures I sent her she couldn't wait to see it and really loved it when I brought her out there the following January! I did good!!

Our address was 5080 South 1200 East in South Ogden and these addresses radiated out from the center of the city so it really was easy to find other addresses.

We had two peach trees and a cherry tree in our back yard and the peach trees would get so loaded with peaches that I had to prop the lower branches up with 2x4s to keep them off the ground! We filled up baskets and tried to give most of them away to neighbors but most of them had their own trees so most got thrown away. We got very few cherries off the one tree as it was a favorited birds and it was too tall to cover with netting.

Utah was the center of the Church of Jesus Christ of Latter Day Saints, otherwise known as Mormons, and we were surrounded by them, being the only non-Mormons in our neighborhood. We became good friends with the Miller family next door but were pretty much avoided by most other Mormon neighbors. In some areas of the city they wouldn't let their kids play with or associate with non-Mormon kids, as a number of my younger airmen would attest to.

There were two young Mormon "Elders" that "proselytized" in our neighborhood, which meant that they went about the neighborhood promoting their faith and tried to convert others (us) to it. They were elders Hall and Washburn and really nice 18 year olds and we sort of took them under our wing during most of our time there. We really enjoyed them stopping by the visit even though they really tried hard to convert us! They sort of became our "other" kids and came to our house a lot to "take a break" From their two year, 24-7 mission. On their church day which consisted of three three-hour services, we would look down at the neighborhood stake house (church) and, sure enough, here they would come, running up the street to our house to take a break with us before the next service. We really missed them when their time there was up.

Senior Master Sergeant Bill Sanders was my go-to guy when I finally started my new assignment there. He was in charge of my weapons training program there and had a desk outside my office. He had been there several years and since he was closely involved in weapons manager responsibilities with my predecessor also, he was indispensable in getting me started in the workings of the fighter wing and what did and didn't need my direct attention.

I had three fighter squadrons (54 F-16s) a gun shop and a weapons release shop to manage and there were approximately 200 weapons people assigned so had my hands full. There wasn't many days where I didn't have at least one meeting with either my weapons NCOs or the Operations Group, the Maintenance Group or the Chiefs Group and so was very easy to get "meetinged out"!

I was very anti-micro management in my leadership style as I believed in allowing my subordinate NCOs and flight chiefs to manage their particular missions and day to day operations as they saw fit and without my constant oversight and I can't recall any instance, in my two years there, where I had to step in and use my rank to solve an issue. I truly was blessed with outstanding junior NCOs in the 388th Fighter Wing!

During the three months I was there before Deb got there, I was constantly off to the mountains either hiking or biking and Utah was so perfect for it. And once the snow flew I was up at the Snow Basin Ski Resort skiing when the opportunity presented itself. I tried snowboarding first but just couldn't get the hang of it and spent several days after, healing my sore butt and arms from constant falls. I readily took to skiing though and loved every minute of it.

At that time Snow Basin was a rather laid back sleepy ski resort and was my very favorite place to ski and it was only a half hour from our house but a couple years later, with the winter Olympics in the Wasatch mountains of Utah coming up, it was completely transformed as a number of events, including the downhill races were held there which meant the end of an affordable place to ski!

While we were stationed at Ramstein AB in Germany we became good friends with John and Sue Hicks as Jesse and their son Nito were playmates and the same age. John, as captain there, was in charge of the weapons logistics office at HQ USAFE and so I often worked in conjunction with him and his people. So what a nice surprise to discover them also stationed at Hill AFB where John was now a Colonel and in charge of the Maintenance Group.

John was African American and Sue was Puerto Rican and probably because of that they had such a different outlook and opinion of things and so was always rather entertaining and hilarious when we spent time with them. John was rather reserved and Sue was fiery and very outspoken and so nothing that came out of her mouth surprised us.

One day I had to go and see him about some issue I was dealing with in the Weapons Release Shop. When I got to his office his secretary said he was in a meeting with his maintenance Chiefs and to take a seat until it was over. Well, he saw me and called me into his office and stood up and gave me a hug! And this was in front of five or six of my fellow Chiefs! They just looked at us rather dumb founded and so was teased a little by them later. That was John though and one of many reasons why I chose him to be the master of ceremonies at my retirement ceremony.

This was considered a great honor in the Air Force and he was thrilled to be given that opportunity.

During the two years in Utah I was still able to maintain my tennis addiction as I met J.R. Merservy on a court one day and since we were about the same skill level we started playing together a couple days a week for most of that time. Either outdoors in the summer or indoors in the winter months so really enjoyed his friendship and our court battles. When I wasn't playing tennis I would either weight lift or jog or bike so always kept in good physical condition.

My retirement was fast approaching and so Deb and I had a decision to make. Stay in Utah or move back home. As much as we liked living in Ogden though, we elected to go home to be near family again after being away so many years. I could have taken a job with one of the military contractors in the area there but just wanted to get away from that kind of life and we couldn't afford to stay there and not work either.

We had our house to sell prior to our move back to Minnesota and were getting ready to list it with the realtor we bought it from. One evening a couple, Roy and Lynn Dow, came to our door and asked if they could buy our house from us! They had been next door looking at our neighbors (the Miller's) house that was on the market but thought it too big. They were then told that we were getting ready to sell and so over they came. They immediately fell in love with the house and so after some friendly negotiating and dinner out with them it was a done deal and we saved a lot on the private sale by not having to pay realtor's fees.

Chapter 34

My Stations and Assignments: 1966 to 1998

Lackland AFB	San Antonio, Texas
Lowry AFB	Denver, Colorado
Eglin AFB	Fort Walton, Florida
Ubon Royal Thai Air Base	Ubon, Thailand
Nellis AFB	Las Vegas, Nevada
Davis Monthan AFB	Tucson, Arizona
Utapao Royal Thailand Air Base	Gulf of Siam, Thailand near Sahahip
Mountain Home AFB	Mountain Home, Idaho
Bitburg AB	Bitburg, Germany
Grand Forks AFB	Grand Forks, North Dakota
Ramstein AB	Ramstein, Germany
Whiteman AFB	Knob Noster, Missouri
King Abdul Aziz AB	Dhahran, Saudi Arabia
Hill AFB	Ogden, Utah

Temporary Duty Assignments

Kaneohe Marine Corps Air Station	Kaneohe, Hawaii
Langley AFB	Hampton, Virginia
Gilze Rijen AB	Netherlands
Camp New Amsterdam	Soesterberg, Netherlands
Leipheim AB	Leipheim, Germany
Ankara	Turkey
Royal Air Force Bentwaters	United Kingdom
Royal Air Force Heyford	United Kingdom
Eskisehir	Turkey
Izmir	Turkey
Al Jaber AFB	Kuwait

Chapter 35

Air Force Retirement Ceremony

Colonel John Hicks presenting my retirement certificate

My retirement ceremony took place July 10th of 1998 in the weapons load training hangar. It wouldn't be official until October 31st and I would still have several weeks of duty afterward but it was still a day that I dreaded. The Air Force was my life and to leave the special bond and camaraderie of those that I trusted with my life throughout all those years would not be easy.

My special guests were CMSgt Pat Berryhill and wife Lynne who were our very good friends from Whiteman AFB, and Col. John Hicks and wife Sue, plus other commanders and dignitaries from around the 388th Fighter Wing including the hill AFB Chiefs Group. None of our family could make it though and was rather disappointed about that but with all the goings on that week we wouldn't have had much time with them anyway.

Following the ceremony I still had a month to go before my terminal leave started so technically was still on duty and as my replacement hadn't arrived yet it was still business as usual. It was rather unsettling this time though in starting to pack up our belongings and preparing for the move back to Minnesota in wondering where our next home would be and whether it would be our final move. We had been through that a number of times before and were accustomed to the routine of it but this time the question mark was larger in that it signified the end of something and the start of something new. But, as before, we had no doubts that we would adjust to whatever our new future would bring.

Retirement Ceremony

Chief Master Sergeant Allen O. Gilbertson
388° Operations Group

Hill Air Force Base, Utah
10 July 1998
1000

Chief Master Sergeant Allen O. Gilbertson
Retirement Script

0940: CMSgt Gilbertson and wife arrive at 388 OG, meet with LTC Hicks

0950: Wife and Guests Escorted to their seats

0955: NARRATOR: Good Morning ladies, gentleman and honored guests. Welcome to the 388 Operations Group. Thank you for joining us for this special occasion: the retirement of CMSgt Allen O. Gilbertson after more than 30 years of dedicated service to our nation.

Honored guests with us today include 388th FW/CC Col Hostage, Chief Gilbertson's wife Debbie and his very good friends CMSgt Pat Berryhill and his wife Lynn, from Wright-Patterson AFB, and Mrs. Sue Hicks

During today's ceremony Lt Col Hicks will award CMSgt Gilbertson the Meritorious Service medal and present him with a retirement certificate and a certificate of appreciation to Mrs. Gilbertson. Additionally Col. Hicks will present CMSgt Gilbertson with a flag of the United States of America. Please rise for the entrance of the official party and remain standing for the National Anthem and the presentation of the Meritorious Service Medal

1000: Entrance of Col Hicks and CMsgt Gilbertson turn to each other, Chief Gilbertson is pinned and salutes are exchanged.

NARRATOR: Please remain standing as Co Hicks officially retires CMSgt Gilbertson and presents him with his certificate of retirement

NARRATOR: Reads the retirement, the letter of appreciation from the president. All are handed to Lt Col. Hicks in a blue folder which he presents to CMSgt Gilbertson. Salutes are exchanged.

NARRATOR: Ladies and gentleman, it is traditional during military retirement ceremonies to recognize the contributions the spouse makes to the successful career of the active duty member. Mrs. Gilbertson will now join her husband as Col Hicks presents her with a certificate of appreciation for her dedication, patience and support during CMSgt Gilbertson's military career. **NARRATOR:** Reads Certificate of Appreciation. Certificate and flowers are presented by Lt Col Hicks.

NARRATOR: ladies and gentleman please be seated. Col Hicks will now make a presentation on behalf of the Weapons Standardization Flt.

Lt Col Hicks: Speaks and presents the Flag Case. Finds something nice to say about Chief Gilbertson

NARRATOR: We will now have a presentation to Chief Gilbertson from Col Oltman, 388th OG/CC FW Chief's Group and the Hill AFB Chief's Group

Col Oltman: Makes presentation to Chief

Chiefs: Make presentation of awards and speak about Chief Gilbertson

NARRATOR: Now we'll hear from CMSgt Gilbertson who will hopefully remember to thank his wife.

CMSgt Gilbertson: Yak Yak Yak

NARRATOR: This concludes the formal portion of today's ceremony. Thank you very much for attending. Please join CMSgt Gilbertson and his wife at the east side of the hangar for refreshments.

Speech given by Col. John Hicks

10 July 1998
Hill AFB, Utah

Introduction:

Welcome Col.Hostage, Col. Dougherty, Col Oltman, Col. Gutschenrittter, Commanders, Chiefs, members of the 388 Fighter Wing, Debbie, family and friends of the Gilbertsons. This is a great American day and we honor one great American, Chief master Sergeant Allen O. Gilbertson. I am deeply honored and humbled to have been chosen by Chief Gilbertson to stand before you and preside over Chief Gilbertson's retirement ceremony. Thank you Chief.

Body of Document:

How do you define 30 years of honorable and faithful service to your country? I will tell you simply in three words: **DUTY- HONOR- COUNTRY.** These words personify Chief Gilbertson's service to our great nation which began in 1966 at Lowry Air Force Base, Colorado. This is where the Chief began his career as a load crew member or 462.

Duty: Chief Gilbertson had 12 assignments in 30 years. Nine of the 12 assignments were from 1966 to 1979. He served from Southeast Asia to Southwest Asia and in Europe. He supported seven different weapon systems, the A-7, F-111, B-52, F-15, F-4, B-2 and F-16. The Chief is one of the last of the Vietnam Era/ he served at Ubon Royal Thai Air Base in 1968 as a load crew member on the F-4 during the Vietnam War. He returned from his tour in Thailand and was stationed at Nellis Air Force Base and separated from the Air Force in 1970 and returned to his home in Minnesota.

During his two year break in service, the Chief got married to his wife, Debbie. They have been married for 26 years and have two children, their son Jesse and their daughter Brandy. However the Chief desired to serve his nation over a civilian career and returned to active duty at Davis-Mothan AFB, Arizona as a load crew member on the A-7.

Then in 1974, the Chief was once again back in Thailand at Utapao Royal Thai Air Base as a load crew member on the B-52.

Honor: I mentioned the two assignments to Thailand because the Chief was stationed there in 1967 and 1974. These were turbulent times for our nation when it was not popular to be a member of the Armed Forces; however Chief Gilbertson wore the Air Force blue proudly because of his love for our nation and his family. The Chief continued to serve our nation honorably as a load-crew member and expediter at Mountain Home Air Force Base, in 1975; then he continued on to Bitburg Air Base in 1976, he was part of the transition team from the F-4 to the F-15 Eagle. Again the Chief moved, this time to the Grand Forks Air Force Base in 1979 to become the NCOIC of the weapons loading section.

In 1985 the Chief moved once again but this time to Ramstein Air Base, Germany. He served in the 86 Tactical Fighter Wing as the Weapons Flight Chief. His talents as a weapons manager was recognized by the USAFE/LGW staff. As a result, in 1986 the Chief was selected to the munitions plans superintendent position on the staff. During this same time my family had the opportunity to meet Chief Gilbertson and his family and we became good friends. By the way Chief, I found some pictures last night of the wine festival we all went to in 1987. **PASS PICTURES TO THE CHIEF.**

Then on 1 May 1994, he achieved the highest enlisted rank of Chief Master Sergeant. The Chief has always been a member of a select group of Air Force members. All the 462's but one that were members of the USAFE/LGW staff from 1986 to 1988 made Chief. This was a select group of dedicated Americans: Chief Dick Vancil, Chief David Kerr, Chief Howard Demotta, Chief (Parky) Davis, Chief Gary Charland, Chief Denny Kalik, and Chief Tom Burns. And in attendance today, Chief Tim Fullagar.

Chief Al Gilbertson was an integral part of this group. Chief Gilbertson along with the other Chiefs established the tone for weapons personnel and were instrumental in making needed changes for the weapons community in the Combat Air Forces. Some of the changes included weapons tester enhancements for the F-16, A-10 and F-15. In addition, they established comprehensive load procedures for cross searching of NATO aircraft and assisted in the development of the new ammunition loading systems and much more. I am honored to have served with each one of you.

After the tour in Europe the Chief was assigned to the B-2 site activation force and the 509th Bomb Wing Weapons Manager, Whiteman Air Force Base. Finally the Chief and I met again in 1996 here at Hill AFB. The Chief is currently the 388 Fighter Wing Weapons manager.

Country: Commitment to our nation first. The notion to lay down his life for our ideals to preserve our way of a life. To ensure freedom for all…….. this is Chief Master Sergeant Gilbertson.

This is how you define 30 years: DUTY-HONOR-COUNTRY. I salute you Chief!!

CHIEF MASTER SERGEANT ALLEN O. GILBERTSON
Air Force Biography

Chief Master Sergeant Allen O. Gilbertson was born in Appleton, Minnesota on February 27, 1948 and grew up on a farm near Montevideo, Minnesota. He graduated from Milan High School in 1966.

Chief Gilbertson enlisted in the Air Force in December 1986 and upon completion of basic training he attended Armament System Training school at Lowry AFB, Colorado for training as a weapons technician on fighter aircraft. In March 1967 he went to the 33 TFW Eglin AFB, Florida for his first assignment where he trained on the F-4D Phantom.

In June 1968 he deployed with the 25th TFS to the 8th TFW Ubon Royal Thai AB, Thailand as an F-4 load crew member. In June 1969 he was assigned to the 57th FWS, Nellis AFB, Nevada as a load crew chief and in December 1970 he separated from Air Force and returned to Minnesota.

Chief Gilbertson returned to active duty in November 1972 and was assigned to the 355th MMS at Davis-Monthan AFB, Arizona as a load crew chief on the A-7D. While there he supported a three month COMMANDO ELITE deployment to Kaneohe, MCAS, Hawaii.

In March 1974 he was assigned to the 307th MMS, Utapao Royal Thai AFB, Thailand as a Load Standardization Crew member on the B-52-D.

In March 1975 he went to the 366th MMS, Mountain Home AFB, Idaho as an F-111F load crew chief and later as a flight line expediter.

He was reassigned to the 36th MMS, Bitburg AB, Germany in July 1976 as an F-4E load team chief and prior to transition to F-15 aircraft he was sent to Langley AFB, Virginia where he trained on the new aircraft and returned to Bitburg AB as a Squadron Lead Crew chief.

In March 1979 he went to the 319th MMS, Grand Forks AFB, North Dakota, first as a B-52H load crew chief, then a flight line expediter, shift supervisor, Quality Control evaluator and finally as NCOIC of the weapons loading section.

He was next assigned to the 86th TFW, Ramstein AB, Germany in September 1985 as a weapons flight chief. He attended NCO Academy at Kaupun, AB, Germany where he was a Distinguished Graduate and upon graduation was selected to a Munitions Plans superintendent position at HQ USAFE/LGW directorate.

In September 1988 he was assigned to the B-52 Site Activation Task Force, Whiteman AFB, Missouri as the first B-2 Armament Systems Superintendent. He attended the Senior NCO Academy at Gunter AFB, Alabama from August to October 1993 and in February 1995 he accepted a core tasking as the Wing Weapons Manager, 4404th Wing, Dhahran, Saudi Arabia. Upon his return to Whitman AFB in June 1995 he was selected as the 509th Bomb Wings Weapons Manager.

In September 1996 he assumed his position as 388th FW Weapons Manager.

He achieved his present rank as Chief Master Sergeant on 1 May 1994. His Military awards and decorations include the Meritorious Service Medal with three devices, Air Force Commendation Medal, Air Force Achievement Medal with one device, Vietnam Campaign Medal, Vietnam Service Medal, Republic of Vietnam Cross of Gallantry Medal, Southwest Asia Service Medal and Small Arms Marksmanship award.

He is married to the former Debra George of Litchfield, Minnesota. They have a son and a daughter, Jesse 22, and Brandy 19.

Chapter 36

Retired Life and a Few More Thoughts

Upon our return home we stayed in my brother Lynn's and his wife Carol's cabin on Lake Minnewaska for almost two months while we house hunted. We found nothing in that area that we liked and started looking for something in the New London/Spicer area. After several weeks there we finally settled on a home on the south side of North Long Lake, they accepted our offer and about a month later we moved in at 13340 208th Ave North East. It was between New London and the small town of Hawick. It needed a whole makeover and after a year of that it was finally very livable. We fell in love with the lake as soon as we saw it and that influenced our decision.

I initially planned on complete retirement but was offered a job at Menards in Belgrade during a shopping trip there, so I took it as I was already getting rather bored of not working.

That job lasted about six months until I was offered a job by Greg Melges at *Mel's Sporting Goods* in Spicer, working his gun department. Since I had a life-long experience with firearms I gladly took the job and worked there for almost five years until I decided to be my own boss and started a painting business at the urging of my cousin Gene Ryer. I still do that to this day.

Tragedy has struck our family too as just months after our move my sister Nancy was killed in a car accident at the age of 52. She left behind a husband and nine children. We were all totally devastated by her death but I believe it hit Dad the hardest. Dad died three years later due to complications of prostate and bone cancer and I also believe, of a broken heart. He was 86.

Over the recent years we have experienced the passing of aunts, uncles, other relatives, friends and neighbors and most recently the huge loss of my nephew Ryan, Ron's oldest son. A snowmobile accident took his life at the age of 41. He was such a large part of so many lives in the family and the Montevideo community and is greatly missed. He had this disarming quiet humor about him that endeared him to so many.

My favorite passion in the fall of the year was pheasant hunting and along with Ron and Ryan, Dustin, John Dalvang, Nathan Molde and three or four dogs we hunted many weekends and were, most days, very successful. I started bringing my grandson Teagan along when he was big enough to walk the miles a day through fields. Like I did when I was a kid, he first started carrying a pellet gun to learn firearm safety, then an unloaded 20 gauge shotgun, then finally he got to go "loaded!" With the passing of Ryan though, hunting just doesn't seem to be so fun anymore.

Jesse and me in the Boundary Waters Canoe Area

Canoe tripping in the Boundary Waters Canoe Area is another of my passions and try to go up there every other year with Jesse for five or six days. I've also been up there with my son-in-law Eric and Teagan. I have always been nature oriented and here I am quoting President Teddy Roosevelt, *"Here is your country. Cherish these natural wonders, cherish the natural resources, cherish the history and romance as a sacred heritage for your children's children. Do not let selfish men or greedy interests skin your country of its beauty, its riches or its romance."*

Mom is now 95 and living comfortably at *Home Front*, an assisted living home, in Montevideo where she has resided since 2008. She has problems with some dementia but otherwise is in good health.

Deb and I are living a quiet life on the lake and enjoy being on the water, on the pontoon along with a cooler of beer!

As of this writing (fall of 2015) my son Jesse and his two sons Thatcher and Oliver live in St. Louis, Missouri and we see them several times a year. My daughter Brandy and her husband Eric Grieger and their son Teagan and daughter Brynn live in Willmar, about 30 minutes away so we see them quite often and attend many of their sporting events.

My List

I can't end this undertaking without revealing the few things to do on my "bucket list" before I die and they are:

1. Do a Polar Plunge. Result – jumped into Green Lake in Jan 2007.
2. Go skydiving! Result – did that at the jump center by Eloy, Arizona in January of 2015 from 13,000ft.
3. Own a Chevrolet Corvette! Result – purchased a Red 2006 Corvette convertible in Montevideo in June of 2015.
4. Finish this book! Result – accomplished!
5. Beat Cancer.

Enjoying Arizona from 13,000 feet at 130 MPH

My 2006 Corvette convertible

After all is said and done, I'll keep on with life enjoying; family, friends, nature, reading action, biographical, military related or historical fiction books. Pheasant hunting, firearms, pontooning on the lake, rock and roll, soul and Motown music, piano music by Jim Brickman, soundtrack music by John Barry and James Horner, muscle cars, Corvettes, the Boundary Waters Canoe Area, genealogy, physical fitness, drag racing, high school basketball, college and pro football, tennis, chocolate, classic movies, beer and last but not least, Lutefisk!

My son asked me, "Dad is your book real narcissistic?" I thought about it for a few days because now it bothered me after losing count of all the "I" and "me" in it and because I shy away from books written in the first person. So with no other method other than to refer to myself as "he" or "said person" then yes it is but I'll just call it "humble" narcissism. There, I am at peace.

In Summary

This is a project that I've worked on for about 12 years. It is as factual as I can be based on my current memories of those many years past. I did this more for my descendants who follow me than for myself although I've taken great enjoyment in the remembering and the telling. I only wished that those who came before me had done the same recording of their life and times. What a treasure that would have been. I hope that my descendants will treasure my life experiences in these pages and take much enjoyment from them and that sometime in their life they tell their own story.

I've heard it said that "we live the life that our ancestors dreamt of" and I believe that for many of us, we dream of living the simple life they lived. We all thought we had the perfect life in our youth. The misfortune of age makes those memories so indispensable. These were the "good old days" and this is my legacy.

Chapter 37

Family Photos

At Mom and Dad's Fiftieth Wedding Anniversary party in 1995

Mom and Dad

Our family in 1996 at the Skordahl reunion in Smith Park in Montevideo

2008 A successful day of pheasant hunting. Kneeling, me and Ron, L-R Dustin Gilbertson, Ryan Gilbertson, Nathan Molde and Todd Dalvang. Photo by John Dahlvang

With my grandson Teagan pheasant hunting near Big Bend, Minnesota

With my brother Lynn on the beach at Fort Myers, Florida 2008

After Dad's Funeral November 2001

My family 2014 Front Row L-R Oliver, Thatcher, Deb, Allen, Brynn, Second Row L-R Jesse, Eric, Teagan, Brandy

Me and Deb